Monetary Revolution USA

Convert the USA to Use Gold as Money
Paper Notes are Just Claim Checks for Gold
Weight of 24 ct Gold is Unit of Account for Pricing
Allow Private Mints with License Optional
Abolish the Fed, USD, and Legal Tender Laws

Author: David Redick

First Edition   January-2010   106 pages
Eleventh Edition (2f)   August-2017   146 pages

Published by: 'Forward USA Foundation',
www.SaferInvesting.org

Library of Congress Control Number: 2009941213
ISBN: 1449904238 , EAN-13: 9781449904234

Printed in the USA by CreateSpace.com, a DBA of On-Demand Publishing LLC, part of the Amazon group of companies.

Other books by Dave: First edition dates are shown, but all books have been updated as needed.

1. **'Restore the USA',** August-2017, 156 p.; Presents a broad range of problems and solutions about the Federal government.

2. **'How to Protect and Grow Your Wealth',** August-2017, 108 p.; Internationalize your assets to avoid decline of the US Dollar, capital controls, and confiscation, and to minimize taxes.

All books are available on Amazon.com.

As with my first book 'Rebuild America Now', this book is dedicated to my daughters, their families, and all others in their generations and beyond, who will inherit the debt, losses, and problems discussed in this book.

I hope my work makes things better for them.

Some seekers of monetary reform want: *'The abolition of central banking and a full separation of money from the state, through a monetary system based on competitive, private, free banking.'* Prof. Richard Ebeling (Citadel.edu) commented on this statement; *'This is the ultimate and most reasonable of all the alternatives to the existing system of monetary central planning through the government institution of central banks.'*

"Give me control of a nation's money and I care not who makes it's laws" –1790, Mayer Amschel Bauer Rothschild

"The only thing necessary for the triumph of evil is for good people to do nothing.", Edmund Burke

"Resistance is not futile, but the most constructive and noble stance of all.", Lew Rockwell

"There are lots of bad governments in this world. The only bad government we have a right or obligation to change is the one in Washington, D.C.", Charley Reese

"Principles are intended *especially* to guide our behavior in difficult times. If they don't do so, then our proclaimed principles stand revealed as having been nothing but rhetoric in the worst sense of the word.", Robert Higgs

"A nation of sheep will beget a government of wolves.", Edward R. Murrow

List of Tables and Figures

Part 1:

"Give me control of a nation's money and I care not who makes it's laws" – 1790, Mayer Amschel Bauer Rothschild (1743 -1812), Founder of the worldwide Rothschild Banking Dynasty

Definition of Revolution: Activity or movement designed to effect fundamental changes in the socioeconomic situation (Merriam-Webster)

Introduction

This book is written to educate a broad audience, from citizens and students, to professors, politicians, and bankers, on what is wrong with our monetary system, and how to fix it.

The USA needs a **Monetary Revolution** to end distortions and losses in our economy, and end corruption in government and the financial services industry. Most of our citizens have accepted the immoral and counterproductive attitude that: 1. The government should and will bail out most people and businesses that get in financial trouble, even if due to irresponsible, self-serving, conduct, and 2. It is proper to tax others (typically 'the rich' and 'corporations') to fund benefits for yourself, which I call gang-theft-by-vote. Federal money feeds these bad habits. The Liberals and Progressives want 'their' politicians to fund their projects (to get their votes), but object when other politicians support subsidies and favors for the 'capitalism and 'corporations' they hate. Of course, 'once the door is opened a bit for the government to 'help' and 'manage' social and business projects, it is pushed wide open by these money and favor seekers! The economic and moral decline of our country and its worldwide empire are the result.

What does our monetary system have to do with this? The key underlying issues are: 1. Internationally, the US dollar is the world's primary reserve currency (while this status lasts), so we are the only nation that can create dollars out of thin air to pay our foreign debts (imports and loans) with our own currency (most nations must buy US Dollars) without facing exchange rates (very handy for our big spending government !), and 2. Our central bank, the Federal Reserve System, creates new fake money to fund the excessive federal spending (politicians like that better than raising taxes), plus recent massive bailouts of firms run by their friends, using phony reasons such as 'too big to fail'. In addition to 'normal' borrowing to fund deficits, our federal debt increases because, 1. Our foreign suppliers often invest in US Treasury securities with the dollars we pay them for our imports, thus making it easier for us to borrow and spend more, and 2. More borrowing and new money is needed because US states become dependent on federal money as they seek and accept grants, pork, and federally funded state projects with strings attached (happily provided by vote-seeking congresspersons). All of this federal spending leads to an excessive increase in our money supply, which causes price inflation and eventual failure of the US dollar as its value drops worldwide. Thus, our present mode of operation is not sustainable and must end.

As my effort to avoid further decline of our USA, this book focuses on problems and solutions about our monetary system, and how we fund government at all levels (city to federal), and banking. My prior book, 'Rebuild America Now', covers other economic and social problems.

Broadly, a 'monetary system' for a nation is the system used to provide and control the exchange of money. It includes the currency (physical coins and paper, or their electronic form; see Glossary), mints, various types of private (not government owned) banks, and usually a 'central bank' which manages the system and stores the nation's reserves (gold, currency of other nations, etc.). In most nations, the central bank is owned and operated by the government, but our Federal Reserve System is a so-called 'private' corporation, but operates in secrecy and kow-tows to pressure from politicians; more on that in Chapter 2. All developed nations today control their monetary systems tightly, including 'legal tender' laws that in various ways force people to use the 'official' government money. History shows us that private money (issued by non-government mints) and banking always works well, where anyone can create money and run a bank, and the only government role is to prevent fraud and theft (see 'Private Gold Standard' on pages 100 and 140, and Core Principle on pages 13, and 139). The crooks that create and push fake money (as in dope 'pushers') are soon discovered and no one will use their money or bank. However, when the government is the crook, and uses legal tender laws to force use of their fake money, it is harder for the citizens to make corrections! Politicians always try to gain control of the system so they can manipulate it to fund projects to keep and enhance their jobs, egos, and power. They make new fiat money out of thin air, debase coins (reduce precious metal content or coin size), etc. 'Fiat' means the government declares the 'face value' of metal or paper money without regard to the market-based value of the material of which it is made. They also borrow money from banks and other nations, usually by selling bonds. Bankers have the same incentive to control government (with loans, bribes and threats), and thus the monetary system, and history shows they have been successful at it. Their favorite method is to control the central bank of a nation, and it is said they arrange 'troubles' (wars, assassinations) for those who won't cooperate. The Rothschild banking family has been preeminent worldwide in starting and controlling central banks. The formative days of banking and securities dealers in the U.S. (through 1930) were dominated by the families of Morgan, Rockefeller, Warburg, Carnegie, Harriman, du Pont, Astor, and Kennedy. Their legacy of government control is still with us.

Thus, the world has a long history of nations that have failed due to abuse of their monetary system to fund wars, excessive spending, and corruption. The failed empires (they had lots of colonies) of Rome, France, Portugal, Spain and England are examples. Sadly, the USA is in the late stage of a failing empire for the same reasons. We don't have colonies, but with our over 800 bases in 130 countries (and growing), we exert a lot of control, which has the same effect. For more on empires, go to this link;

Given those historical trends, where are we today? It is not surprising that our monetary system, and those in most of the world, are controlled by corrupt politicians, securities dealers (aka 'Wall Street'), and bankers. Learned economists join the group-thought to have secure jobs. The greed and treachery of these financial industry leaders and their willing dupes caused the world depression that started in 2007 and is still unfolding as I write in February, 2013. Greed is a human trait and present wherever humans operate, and in any type of political or economic system (Capitalism, Socialism, 'Progressive', Fascism, Communism; see Glossary). Crooked leaders and their gangs are worst in the latter four more centralized and authoritarian systems, where the authority of government, and its fake money, protect their jobs and feed their growth. When these self-serving people get control of a government, and a country's financial system, major distortions, wars, and then economic and moral failure, always occur.
This book will analyze where we are today, and offer a plan on how we can repair the damage and recover.
The purpose of my work and books is to promote a form of government that creates more liberty, peace, prosperity, justice and morality. I find that free-market capitalism (all voluntary, and run by willing buyers and sellers, no government 'favors' to 'crony pals') is best. All of my recommendations comply with my

core principle: "The government's proper role is to **protect** the personal and property rights of its citizens and legal residents, as **individuals**, from threat to, or violation of, their rights **by others**". Our Constitution supports this approach.

For more information, and updates on topics herein, see my web site www.SaferInvesting.org. To see my essays on this, and other topics, go to my archive at ActivistPost.com, scroll to bottom of Home page and select 'Contributors', then my name.
Please send comments to RedickD@aol.com.

Thanks for your interest and support, Dave Redick

Dave's Brief Bio (see page 142 for details)

Personal and Education:
1935: Born in MI (near Detroit)
1958: BS-Engineering, University of Michigan, Ann Arbor, MI
1965: MBA-Economics, Santa Clara University, Santa Clara, CA

Career:
1958 -1969: Aerospace Engineering and hi-tech sales
1970 -2004: Telecommunications sales and management
1993 -2000: VP Sales then CEO of consultant HNTelecom.com
2000 -2001: VP and Cofounder of $6 mill. venture capital funded startup Fiberstreet.com (closed, use Google)
2004 - Present: a) Speaker and Author on Economics, Better Government, and Trends, and b) Energy Consultant

Politics: Active in 'limited government and sound money' political work since 1978. Candidate for US Congress (3 times), and State Assembly (2).

Chapter 1: The US Monetary System

A Brief History of Money

Various material of value (shells, hoes, tobacco) have been used as money, and all served the need for a medium of exchange, unit of account, and a store and measure of value, but gold always emerges as best, as described below (see p.91). People made token coins of base metal (not rare or precious) for local use. Metal objects were introduced as money around 5,000 B.C. By 600 BC, the Lydians (now part of Turkey) became the first in the Western world to make metal coins of a certain weight, fineness (purity), and shape. Their **Stater** was made of electrum, a naturally occurring mixture of gold and silver. The Arabs used the gold **Dinar**, which is still in use. Greece used the silver **Drachma**. The Byzantine **Solidus** (meaning 'solid') **gold** coin, which evolved to the **Bezant**, was introduced by Emperor Constantine I, in 312 AD, permanently replacing the **Aureus** as the gold coin of the Roman Empire. The Bezant was about 4.5 grams of 23 ct gold, and was maintained essentially unaltered in weight, dimensions and purity for 600 years. This stability of value was a key factor in the prosperity of those times. For more on old coins, see;
http://en.wikipedia.org/wiki/List_of_historical_currencies.

Some of the earliest known paper money was about AD 960 in China. This money, made of material with little or no market value when not used as money, was often abused by over-production and became worthless (sounds familiar today!). The world's first central bank was the Bank of England, founded in 1694. It was a privately owned bank, but was given special privileges by the King, such as buying royal bonds with their paper notes. At first, the notes were redeemable in specie (gold or silver), but excessive creation of 'notes' soon started, redeemability ended, and their value dropped. In 1699 King William III appointed physicist Sir Isaac Newton as Master of the Mint to develop rules for management of the banks' money. Newton developed what we now call the Classical Gold Standard with paper notes, or base-metal token coins, redeemable in a certain weight and purity of gold at the issuing bank or mint, by bearer on demand. The rules started in 1707, but were again soon broken and price inflation followed. The British Pound still survived as a 'good as gold' coin and the world's reserve currency until 1914 when they suspended gold redemption so they could inflate the money supply to pay for WW1. The Bank of England was nationalized into a central bank in 1946.

In the USA

The American colonies created 'colonial scrip' (paper currency not backed by a commodity such as gold). It worked well for a few years but it was abused by excessive expansion of supply (monetary inflation) in some areas, and became worthless. This gave our Founders fair warning about the problems with paper money. The King of England frowned on their attempts at monetary independence and their scrip was banned by English Parliament in the 'Currency Act of 1764'. This caused a depression in the colonies, and was one of the reasons for the American Revolution. Notice that this is not in the government-approved history books in our schools!

The Colonies and early U.S. used many types of currency from other nations, and had no 'official' U.S. money. The 'Spanish Milled Dollar' (or '8 Reales') was prominent due its known silver content (averaged 27.47 grams of 0.93 fine silver, but varied with mint and date; Wiki). People often cut these coins into pie-slice shaped halves, quarters, and eighths (or 'bits') to make change. These are the famous "pieces of eight", and '2 bits' equals a quarter dollar.

Following Alexander Hamilton's recommendations to create a national currency, Congress enacted the 'Coinage Act of 1792' (The Mint Act). It established gold and silver as the monetary standards of the United States with the gold set at 15 times the value of silver. This fixed 'bi-metallic' standard caused trouble later! The initial US silver dollar coins were struck of 26.96 grams of 0.8924 fine silver (alloyed with copper). The diameter was 39 to 40 millimeters with a lettered edge reading 'HUNDRED CENTS ONE DOLLAR OR UNIT'. The act also allowed for the creation of a national mint. It was the world's first decimal-based monetary system.

Between the adoption of the Constitution and the Civil War the United States government did not issue paper money as we know it today, but on many occasions it did issue short term debt called Treasury Notes. They also issued Demand Notes that were intended to function as money, and were authorized within the legal framework of Treasury Notes. This was a 'sneaky' ploy since the U.S. was not generally assumed to have the authority to issue banknotes at that time.

The Continental Congress had issued Continental dollars between 1775 and 1779 to help finance the American Revolution. The paper Continental dollars nominally entitled the bearer to an equivalent amount of Spanish Milled dollars but were never redeemed in silver and lost 99% of their value by 1790 despite the American victory. Some claim that British General Howe printed thousands of Continentals and sold them cheaply in order to destroy its value. With the fate of the Continentals in mind, the Founding Fathers put no provision for a paper currency in the Constitution, and they forbaide the states to use anything but gold or silver as legal tender. As a result, the pre-Civil War circulation of banknotes in the United States consisted of private issues, including issues by private federally chartered banks such as the First and Second banks of the U.S. (more below). The Coinage Act of 1834 set gold at 16 times the value of siver, which undervalued the silver, causing traders to export it for use abroad.

In 1861 Lincoln needed money to finance the so-called 'Civil War' (actually a war of aggression against the South, which had the right to secede, to retain them as a source of cotton, and a market for Northern manufactured goods; see page 131), so he went with his Secretary of the Treasury to New York to apply for the necessary loans. The Bankers (money changers), wishing the Union forces to fail, offered loans at annual rate of 24% to 36%. Lincoln declined the offer. An old friend of Lincoln's, Colonel Dick Taylor of Chicago, was put in charge of solving the problem of how to finance the war. His solution is recorded as this: "Just get Congress to pass a bill authorizing the printing of full legal tender treasury notes... and pay your soldiers with them and go ahead and win your war with them also." The initial 'Greenbacks' were redeemable in gold or silver, but redemption soon ended so the Legal Tender Act of 1862 was issued to force people and firms to accept them. Next came the National Bank Acts of 1863 and 1864 that created a system of federally chartered 'national' banks that issued bank notes supplied by the new 'Office of the Comptroller of the Currency' (OCC) and US Mint (both part of the Department of the Treasury). The Acts also put a ten percent tax on state-issued bank notes, which ended their money-making and gave us the first federal monopoly on money creation! The Secret Service was also created, so only DC could make counterfeit money! (more on P. 61)

Silver Coins and Certificates

The next major banking law was the 'Fourth Coinage Act of 1873' led by Pres. Grant that demonetised silver and effectively put the US on the gold standard, which replaced the fixed-ratio gold and silver bimetallic standard that had been created by Alexander Hamilton. Many of the poorer citizens saw this as a "crime" because it devalued their silver, which then prompted passage of the Bland-Allison Act by Congress on February 28, 1878. It did not provide for the "free and unlimited coinage of silver" demanded by Western miners, but it did require the United States Treasury to purchase up to $4 million of silver bullion from mining companies in the West, to be minted into coins that would be legal tender for all debts, like gold. Paper 'Silver Certificate' money was first issued in 1878 and bore the words; 'Silver Certificate, This certifies that there is on deposit in the Treasury of the United States of America 'x' Dollars in silver payable to the Bearer on Demand', and 'This Certificate is Legal Tender for all Debts, Public and Private.' Most were $1, $2, and $5. Redemptions were paid in $1 silver coins (0.8 ounces of 90% pure silver).

The Gold Standard Act of 1900 ended bi-metalism (a fixed ratio of gold to silver value), and required the US Mint must hold only 40% gold reserves to redeem notes. The bankers conspired to get the Federal Reserve System approved on December 23, 1913 (see page 21). Today's 'Federal Reserve Notes' only bear the words 'This Note is Legal Tender for all Debts Public and Private. JFK was planning to bypass the Fed by having the Treasury issue 'U.S. Notes' (certificates redeemable in silver) and silver coins. Some say this led to his death.

The Morgan silver dollar coin (1878-1921), and the Peace (1921-1935) had 0.8 oz of 0.9 purity, thus 0.72 oz; four quarters or ten dimes had the same total, and all had wide usage. Pres. Johnson approved the 'Coinage Act of 1965' which ended silver content in coins (their bullion market value had exceeded their face value), thus 1964 and prior coins (known as 'junk' silver due to wear) were 'hoarded' and valued for their silver content. Now the quarter is

91.67 percent copper and 8.33 percent nickel. Pennies are 97.5% zinc and 2.5% copper. The exception was the Kennedy half dollar which started in 1964 as a memorial (he died on Nov. 22, 1963) with 90% silver (0.362 oz), then 40% in 1965-70 and zero from 1971 until now. The Eisenhower silver dollar in 1971-78 had 0.316 oz. Redemption for metal of Silver Certificates ended in Oct-1967, but they remain legal tender. See P. 117 for more. Nixon abrogated the Bretton Woods Agreement in August, 1971, ending all US money ties to precious metal.

The Petrodollar System

The 1971 floating, goldless, USD was saved by the **Petrodollar System, a paper crutch!**. The deal is explained in this excerpt from a Jan-2012 article by Marin Katusa of www.CaseyResearch.com; "*In 1973, President Nixon and Sec. Kissinger asked King Faisal of Saudi Arabia to accept only US dollars as payment for oil and to invest any excess profits in US Treasury bonds, notes, and bills. In exchange, Nixon pledged to protect Saudi Arabian oil fields from the Soviet Union and others. It was the start of something great for the US, and is the foundation for the value of the USD.*

By 1975 all of the members of OPEC agreed to sell their oil only in US dollars. Every oil-importing nation in the world started saving their surplus in US dollars so as to be able to buy oil; with such high demand for dollars the currency strengthened. On top of that, many oil-exporting nations like Saudi Arabia spent their US dollar surpluses on Treasury securities, providing a new, deep pool of lenders to support US government spending." For the entire article, visit: (http://www.caseyresearch.com/cdd/demise-petrodollar.

Notice that the Oil Embargo, related to the Yom Kippur War, started in 1974. OPEC demanded, and got, price increases to $12.20 bbl in 1975 and $25 by 1979 (but this only accounted for inflation since the $2.77 price in 1948; it had been only $3.50 in 1973!!). The Petrodollar system continues today, and remains a key support of the USD. One of the reasons the US invaded Iraq and Libya (and is threatening Iran) was that their leaders had started selling oil for gold and other currencies; a death warrant! Other reasons are; 1) getting their oil and denying it to China, and 2) Israel. Based on recent gold purchases, and China's May-2014 US$400 bn purchase of gas (may be paid in yuan) from Russia, China and Russia might be planning to destroy the petrodollar system by using their own money, and thus help crash the U.S. economy by ending the USD's role as a reserve currency? (More on P. 59)

US Central Banks

Politicians like central banks that control the national monetary system because they can manipulate them to gain funding without politically unpopular taxation. In 1791, the 'First Bank of the United States', (BUS-1), was started, but it failed in 1811. The second attempt was the 'Second Bank of the United States' (BUS-2), which was chartered in 1816, with a renewal required in 1836.

"The predominant reason that the Second Bank of the United States was chartered was that in the War of 1812, the U.S. experienced severe inflation and had difficulty in financing military operations. The Second B.U.S. was in no sense a federal-national bank but rather a privately held banking corporation. The bank had a unique relationship (special deals, monopolies, etc.) with the federal government that gave it access to substantial profits. President Andrew Jackson strongly opposed the renewal of

the 'second' bank's charter, and built his platform for the election of 1832 around doing away with the Second Bank of the United States, which he did in Sep-1833."
(wikipedia.org)

The Whig Party (which liked 'big government', and included the young, ambitious, Abe Lincoln) was started to oppose Jackson's termination of BUS-2, but it failed.

Creating the Fed

The Federal Reserve System should be considered the third U.S. central bank (BUS-3). The secret plan to create the financial monster now known as the 'Fed' was consummated on November 22, 1910 at a private club on Jekyll Island, Georgia. Congregated at his clandestine meeting were some of the most powerful political and financial people in Europe and America including:

Nelson W. Aldrich: Republican "whip" in the Senate, chairman of various committees including the Committee on Finance and Chairman of the National Monetary Commission. Aldrich was a business associate of J. P. Morgan and father-in-law to John D. Rockefeller, Jr.

Frank Vanderlip: President of the National City Bank of New York, which at the time was one of the most powerful banks in the US and was under the control of William Rockefeller and the international investment banking house of Kuhn, Loeb & Company. His 1935 book 'From Farmboy to Financier' revealed the secret events on Jekyll Island.

A. P. Andrew: Assistant Secretary of the U.S. Treasury

Henry P. Davison: Senior Partner of J. P. Morgan Company, emissary of J. P. Morgan

Charles D. Norton: President of the Morgan-dominated First National Bank of New York

Benjamin Strong: Head of J. P. Morgan's Bankers Trust Co. and loyal lieutenant of J. .P Morgan

Paul Warburg: A recent émigré from Germany, partner in the banking firm of Kuhn, Loeb & Co. who was the agent of the German Central Bank (Reichsbank) and the Rothschilds and Warburgs banking dynasties based in Europe. He wrote a book about how they contrived passage by Congress and approval by Pres. Wilson.

*'The sole intention of these conspirators was to draft a blueprint for a strong central bank that served their interests. This blueprint was the **Federal Reserve System** and the prize was the future control of the money supply and credit of the United States.*
*Because the Federal Reserve System was to be a bank of issue then, just as the plotters understood all too well, it was **unconstitutional from its inception**.*
(www.overlordsofchaos.com)

Aldrich headed a commission in 1911 to study the role and need for central banks. He came home from a study trip to Europe claiming to be a new supporter of them, but that was a ploy to cover the existing plans from Jekyll Island in 1910. The Aldrich Commission's report was submitted to Congress in 1912. Although Woodrow Wilson, a Democrat, won the 1912 election, the Republican Aldrich's plan shaped the extensive debate that followed. A Democrat, Carter Glass of Virginia, shepherded the Federal Reserve Act through the Congress. On Dec. 23, 1913, when many Congresspersons, including major opponents of central banking, had already left town, Congress adopted the Federal Reserve Act, also known as the Owens-Carter Act. Even the name was meant to deceive, so they chose:

1. 'Federal' to make it seem to be part of the government, and 2. 'System' instead of 'Bank' because many Congresspersons opposed a federal bank. They planned the 'system' with twelve regional banks (each a privately owned corporation) to satisfy private bankers that their regional concerns would be heard.

Fake 'Mandates' and the 'Real Reasons' the Fed was Created

A further fake 'selling point' to gain support from the people and Congress was to declare that the 'dual mandate' of the Fed was to maintain; 1. Stable value of the Dollar, and 2. High employment, and the Fed has failed at both! **The fake mandates shielded the 'real' reasons of; 1. A 'flexible' source of new money for politicians to spend (causing price inflation, a hidden tax), and 2. The 'lender of last resort' role to bail out banks and other firms with good political connections! This, and other government meddling, led to the 'casino banking' that caused the 2008 crash, with more to come in 2013 and up.**

'The "unprecedented speed" with which the Federal Reserve Act had been passed by Congress during what became known as "the Christmas massacre".
Bernard Baruch, a principal contributor to Wilson's campaign fund, was stunned when he was informed that Wilson refused to sign the bill. So he assured Wilson that his concerns were a minor matters, which could be fixed up later through "administrative processes". With this reassurance, Wilson signed the Federal Reserve Act on December 23, 1913. **History proved that on that day, the Constitution ceased to be the governing covenant of the American people.'** (from www.goldismoney.info)

Structure of the Fed

'*The Federal Reserve System consists of the Board of Governors (*The US President appoints the seven members of the Board and they serve for 14 years. The chairman and vice-chairman are chosen by the President from among the sitting Governors for four-year terms. **Thus political independence is a joke!***) the 12 Federal Reserve banks, the Federal Open Market Committee, the Federal Advisory Council, and, since 1976, the Consumer Advisory Council. There are also within the system several thousand member banks. The Board of Governors of the Federal Reserve System, domiciled in Washington DC, determines the reserve requirements of the member banks within statutory limits, reviews and determines the discount rates established by the 12 Federal Reserve banks, and reviews the budgets of the reserve banks.*

Each Federal Reserve Bank is a privately owned corporation established pursuant to the Federal Reserve Act of 1913 *to supposedly serve the public interest. A board of nine directors governs each Federal Reserve Bank, six of whom are appointed by the member banks and three of who are appointed by the Board of Governors of the Federal Reserve System. The **12 Federal Reserve banks** are located in Boston, New York, Philadelphia, Chicago, San Francisco, Cleveland, Richmond, Atlanta, St. Louis, Minneapolis, Kansas City and Dallas. Determination of Federal Reserve Bank policy in the purchase and sale of securities on the open market is the power of the Federal Open Market Committee (FOMC) consisting of the seven members of the Board of Governors and five members elected by the Federal Reserve banks. The supreme regulatory powers in fiscal affairs gifted to this private monopoly called the Federal Reserve System manifest in several ways but the most important are the instruments of so-called direct or indirect control.*
1. Of direct control, one method used is adjusting the legal reserve ratio (i.e. the proportion of its deposits that a member bank must hold in its reserve account) thereby increasing or reducing the amount of new loans that the commercial banks

can make. Thus, in this way the potential money supply is expanded or reduced because loans give rise to new deposits.
2. Another direct control mechanism to influence potential money supply is by the manipulation of the discount (rediscount) rate, which is the rate of interest charged by Federal Reserve banks on short-term secured loans to member banks. Loans are usually sought to maintain reserves at their required level, and so an increase in the cost of such loans has an effect similar to that of increasing the reserve requirement.
3. Of indirect control, the classic method is through open-market operations. It was first used in the 1920s but is now employed daily to make small adjustments in the market. This control mechanism has the Federal Reserve Bank selling or purchasing securities on the open markets that causes a reduction or increase the size of commercial-bank reserves. That is, when the Federal Reserve sells securities, the purchasers pay for them with checks drawn on their deposits, thereby reducing the reserves of the banks on which the checks are drawn'
4. A supplemental control mechanism occasionally used by the Federal Reserve Board is that of changing the margin requirements involved in the purchase of securities.' (from www.overlordsofchaos.com)

Notice that the word 'reserve' is used extensively above, both in the name of the Fed, and its activities. This is because if a private bank gets low on reserves (compared to the legal requirements at the time), it can't make new loans, and this could be widespread in bad economic times. While a new bank depends on investments by shareholders for its initial reserves, profits and borrowing from the Fed become major sources as it grows. Hence, the Fed's role in loaning banks money to boost their reserves is a powerful tool in 'managing' the level of economic activity nationwide. It also allows the Fed, as 'lender of last resort', to do bail-outs in bad times!

The above description shows how the so-called 'privately owned' Fed bank controls the US monetary system. Not mentioned, is that most of its meetings and actions are secret, even to Congress, and that it is heavily politicized and controlled by the Federal government. It was annoying to see the liar Bernanke plead that Rep. Ron Paul's bill HR-1207 (paul.house.gov; retired Jan-2013) to audit the Fed would reduce its independence. What a joke! He really wants the right to secrecy to help his 'friends'!

Nelson Hultberg (www.AFR.com) said it well in his essay 'The Fed is a Fascist Cartel': *"The Federal Reserve, in my opinion, should not be classified as a private corporation. It should be termed a government-run fascist cartel. There are several important reasons for this. For example,*
1. All nationally chartered banks in the Federal Reserve system are forced *by the government to join the cartel.*
2. Bernanke and his board of governors are appointed by the President and approved by the Senate.
3. The Federal Reserve came into being because of an act of Congress, and it can be altered or legislated out of being at anytime by Congress.

These factors are not how private corporations are created or operated. The Fed entails government involvement *in a massive way. Without the special monopoly privileges legislated by Congress that sustain the Fed, it disappears."*

But take heart! It's never too late to abolish the Fed and return to the proven gold standard. Due to rapidly increasing lack of confidence in the Fed since the crash started in 2008, in Nov-2010 a ground swell of support for the gold standard erupted. Here are three examples;

1. Over the weekend of November 6-7, 2010, World Bank president, Robert Zoellick, proposed, in a column written for the Financial Times, that the global economy once more be linked to gold as an anchor to help maintain currency stability and reduce inflationary expectations in international markets. He soon 'clarified' his comment, but the uproar had started!,

2. On November 9, 2010, Dr. Richard Ebeling, Professor of Economics at Northwood University (Northwood.edu), posted the article **'A Return to the Gold Standard?'** in the Daily Bell (dailybell.com) commenting on Mr. Zoellick's statement. Dr. Ebeling wrote; *'At one point in his article, Martin Wolf mentions that some have called for an even more radical monetary reform than even a government-managed new gold standard:* **the abolition of central banking and a full separation of money from the state, through a monetary system based on competitive, private free banking.** *Wolf sets that alternative aside as well, thinking that the world is certainly not ready for such a change, even if it was workable. But, in fact,* **this is the ultimate and most reasonable of all the alternatives to the existing system of monetary central planning through the government institution of central banks.***'*

For a detailed plan for conversion of our fiat 'Fed Note' and coin system to use of gold as money, which includes a form of Prof. Ebeling's plan for allocation of U.S. gold to redeem Fed Notes and coins, refer to my 'Five Step Plan' on page 99. The plan was in the 1st edition of this book in Jan-2010.

There is a growing movement to end corrupt government. Young people are getting concerned. We must **Fight On!**

Chapter 2: Effects of the Fed and Other Central Banks

The Impact of Fake Money

You won't read the following analysis in the newspapers or in a college economics course. Most government and industry leaders, and professors like the present system because their jobs, grants, and social life depend on having and supporting it! This requires an ethical lapse where the fake nature of the money is ignored in order to gain a personal advantage from it They want to be viewed as 'normal', not a radical 'gold bug' who respects the importance of sound money which means gold or silver coins, and paper notes redeemable in gold by anyone, on demand.

The creation of fiat 'official' government money has had a profound effect in history and on our nation and the world today. 'Fiat' means it is worth whatever the government says it is (its 'face value'), although the material of which it is made may have more or less market value (examples: valuable silver dollars and worthless paper, both declared worth $1, and today's American Eagle bullion coin with a 'face value' of $50 for one ounce of gold!).

KEY POINT ! Normally, when a nation creates too much fake money, sellers avoid it for payment, or stop buying its bonds, due to the falling value of both, and the party is soon over. However**, the US is in a unique position never seen in the history of the world**. Our fiat paper money is the primary de facto (not 'formal', since 1971) world's 'reserve currency' (1. anyone will accept it for payment, and keep it as cash, or as a dollar-denominated asset; 2. over 60% of world transactions use it, thus banks keep large reserves of it). Thus, we can create new money (paper or electronic) out of thin-air by the billions and sellers of goods and services worldwide (and in the U.S.) will accept it, and we can pay our debts with it, even as the federal government spends to excess. **No other country can do that!!** We have abused the 'privileged' status of the U.S. dollar (USD) in many immoral and counterproductive ways. It is the underlying cause (funder) of our major problems with jobs (exported due to excessive imports of goods), banking and securities (strange deals based on loose money), excessive personal spending and debt (borrow, buy and play now, pay later!), and expensive wars.

Table 1
The Honest National Debt and Unfunded Liabilities

A, $ 18.406 tn National Debt (disclosed debt)

B.	56,740	Key Misc. unfunded Liabilities (not disclosed
	27,563	Medicare A, B, and D (unfunded)
	14.366	Social Security (unfunded)

$ 98.669 trillion   Total for B

$ 117,075 trillion = Grand Total (A+B)

(Source: USDebtClock.org, Oct. 14, 2015)

The 'official' government debt figures ignore the above Medicare, Soc. Sec. and Misc. items (treated as 'off-budget' !!), plus potential trillions that loom due to $5.3 tn losses at Fannie and Freddie, now government-owned. There are other 'Misc.' items, such as food stamps, not shown above.

The deceit is exposed by the fact that after Congress increased the federal debt limit to $12.104 tn in Feb-2009 (80% of GDP), in Feb-2010 increased it to $14.3 tn, and in Jan-2012 to $16.4 tn (102% of GDP) which was approached in Dec-2012 stirring the 'fiscal cliff ' chaos! On Jan. 23, 2013 they suspended the legal limit on government borrowing until May 19, then agreed on the increase. In Feb., 2014 they agreed to more spending, with no limits, until March, 2015!! Government accounting is loaded with hypocrisy. They ignore the normal accounting rules and honesty that apply to mere citizens, in order to hide the problems they have created. They prosecute private firms for doing the same thing! Note that the above figures do not count the trillions for Obama's health plan!

In 1970 the national debt was $380.9 bn (about $3.4 tn in 2015 dollars), and 37.6% of the GDP. As of Oct. 14, 2015 the national debt was $18.4 tn, and 103% of GDP, thus reaching the danger level of more than GDP!! For definitions of GDP and GNP see p. 139; the government now prefers to use GNP. No one believes the debt will ever be paid. To eliminate it, we can; 1) Increase taxes a lot, 2) Do an overt default (repudiation), and refuse to pay most of it (a serious possibility; Russia and Brazil did!), or 3) Create new fake money (the IMF 'SDR'?), but this would likely cause hyper price inflation, and destroy the US dollar and economy. Horrible choices, all thanks to irresponsible government leaders.

Of course consumer debt (cars, home mortgages – first and second -, credit cards, TVs, etc.) zoomed upward because of the easy (lax terms, sub-prime), cheap (low interest) fake money created by the Fed in 2000 to 2007. As more people lose their jobs, more bills go unpaid, and the defaults and foreclosures are now doing the upward zoom. Sad.

New fiat money, and lax terms, funded the debt explosion. This excessive credit creates and feeds the abusive and corrupt Wall Street and Main Street excessive spending and debt. One cannot underestimate the importance of our ability to pay debts to other nations, and not be required to convert to their money. We can simply create new dollars to pay our debts, with only a minor impact on its value in the short-term. Conversely, other nations must buy dollars (or Euros) to pay for most imports or loans, and face declining exchange rates if they have expanded their money supply too much. We have abused this 'reserve' status and in mid-2010 other nations started seeking alternatives (yuan, yen, a 'basket of currencies', etc.). Most people are not aware that the 'reserve' currency is used for most payments between other nations (example: India pays Brazil for coffee with USD). Hence, all nations keep a supply of USD to use in trade. All banks are required to have sufficient 'reserves' to show a strong asset base for the bank's obligations (mainly demand and time deposits). Since the USD has been valued by the world system as 'good as gold', it is known as a 'reserve currency' and used instead of gold to fund these bank reserves. The Dollar has been used in about 80% of international transactions since its ascendancy in the 1920's (the English 'Pound Sterling faded), but it has become weaker since 2000, and declined to 60% or less in 2012.

About 30% of international deals are now done in Euros, Swiss francs and Yen, but that is increasing as the economies and currencies of China and others grow stronger. Indeed, China started using its yuan for international transactions in mid 2010, and also allowed foreign firms to create a yuan-denominated private equity funds. There was a 13-fold increase in trades settled in yuan in the first half of 2011 from the prior year. This outweighs the potential cost of an unfavorable move in the yuan-dollar exchange rate.

While 'inflation' of the money supply (like a balloon) reduces the value of every US dollar, the US government prefers this to deflation because 'free money' from inflation helps pay off federal debts to other nations. In the extreme, this is a form of default, since the lender gets paid in near-worthless paper money. In mid-2010, our lenders (China, etc.) voiced concern about this possibility.

The federal funds target interest rate were at historic lows of about 1% during 2001 to 2005, which was done to stimulate recovery after the 'dot-com' bubble burst on NASDAQ in March-2000. In Jan-2006 Fed Chairman Greenspan increased interest rates to 5.25%, some say 'to put the brakes on'. The U.S. economy started failing because many banks and Wall Street firms were highly leveraged (over 25:1) in risky investments and could not tolerate losses caused by the rate increases.

During the 2000 to 2007 boom times, Wall Street had been 'securitizing' bundles of various weak and bad debt instruments (subprime mortgages, credit card debt, student loans, etc.) into 'mortgage-backed securities' (MBS), then getting their complicit rating agencies (Moodys, Standard and Poors -S&P-, Fitch) to falsely label them AAA, an act of fraud. By doing so, they could sell them worldwide to get them off their books, and then make more money by making new loans to other weak borrowers. Finally, in Jan-2013 the government filed a law suit against S&P for fraud.

Massive amounts of cheap fake money, supplied by the Federal Reserve System started and supported these debacles. More money was created for Bush's $700 billion TARP program (Troubled Asset Relief Program) in 2008, with the Fed pouring about $2.2 trillion into the economy for their bailouts (the 'Bernanke Spike'), and then $787 bill. more for Obama's Feb-2009 Recovery plan. It's like pouring gas on a fire! This combined $2.987 trillion is now called 'Quantitative Easing-1', or 'QE-1', and showed meager results. Then in Nov-2010 the Fed announced QE-2 to buy $600 billion in long-term U.S. Treasury bonds, ostensibly to push down long-term interest rates, and in Sep-2012 QE-3 to spend $40 bn. per mo. on mortgage-based securities, plus the existing 'Operation Twist' of $45 bn. mo.(to buy and sell short- and long-term US bonds - hence the 'twist - to reduce interest rates), with no end date! The US monetary base has grown from $848 bn in 2008, to a horrible $4, tn in Oct-2014!

Bernanke specialized in study of the 'Great 1930's Depression' for his doctoral program. He claimed that the Fed should have increased the money supply in 1929 when the depression started, instead of reducing it. He was determined to not let that mistake happen again, so he flooded the economy with new money in 2008! As of Nov-2014, results have been disappointing as unemployment gets worse and prices rise. So much for fixing by flooding.

Thomas G. Donlan, Editorial Page Editor of 'Barron's' (Barrons.com) said it well in Oct-2010; *'TARP is just part of a bailout-and-stimulus program that is a huge loser. The government has borrowed money and shoveled it out the window for more than two years. A little of it has leaked back in under the door.'*

Most of our current economic problems were created by the Fed (with cheering from Congress) by flooding the nation with cheap, fake, money as a stimulant since the early '90s. It should surprise no one that people, bankers, and Wall Street reacted by seeking high-return, risky investments (derivatives, etc.) to help them beat the price inflation caused by this easy money (low interest, lax terms), and excessive expansion of the money supply. A second cause of seeking excessive profits and risk was the 'moral hazard' of knowing they would probably be bailed out by the Fed if they got in trouble. Since its creation in 1913, and with a surge since 2000, the Fed has expanded ('inflated') the money supply by twenty times. 'Price Inflation', a secondary effect caused by inflating the money supply, has reduced the US dollars' (USD) purchasing power by 95% (20:1) since 1913, So much for government management !

Many people claim that 'unfettered free-market Capitalism' was the cause of the 2008 crash, and call for more regulation. In fact, we have 'crony capitalism' where the government and businesses exchange favors, and the people lose! Liberal want those favors for their own projects, so they falsely blame '**Capitalism**'. In fact, **Capitalism is just an 'economic system' based on private ownership, free enterprise, and minimal regulation**. Capitalism offers more than economic results, **it is a moral system** that depends on the activity of willing buyers and sellers within the rule of law, not coercion and control by others (the government power folks). Socialists, Liberals, and Progressives have distorted the meaning to call it a 'social system based on greed and power for the rich'. They blame 'corporations' for most of the abuse, while ignoring that in any system (government, church, club, etc.), concentrated power and self-serving, unethical people are always the cause. What they also ignore, through ignorance or bias, is that we have not had a free market since 1913 (when the Fed was born), and worse since 1933 when FDR declared that the government was our mother and boss, and responsible to provide convenience and security for all, and have 'someone else' (the government or 'the rich') pay for it. This pushed a dagger into the heart of our

34

citizen's sense of ethics and personal responsibility, and gave birth to 'crony capitalism'. Now Liberals tout 'shared responsibility' or 'the rich were just lucky, so should pay more' as their basis for taxing others to fund their projects (health, welfare, education, etc.). They forget (or don't know) that the top 1% (by income) of citizens have 20% of the income and pay 38% of the taxes, while 51% of lower income people pay none. Liberals grab for a higher percent but ignore that 'dollars paid' is what counts (have you ever paid for something with 'percent'?), and on this basis of 38-to-1, 'the rich' are already paying more than 'their share'. Our nation's culture and economy have been sliding downhill ever since Progressive Taxation started. Unconstitutional government programs and intervention in the free market have caused our problems. This result shows in every country run by central authority in history, and worldwide today.

History shows us that free market capitalism always provides more liberty, peace, prosperity, morality, and justice for all. I recognize that people violate ethics and justice under capitalism, but this relates to bad people and can occur in any economic system (or church or club). Capitalism still comes out best. Centralized systems such as Socialism give more power to the bad guys.

The Fed's Record of Results

The purchasing power (value) of the US dollar (USD) has dropped by more than 95% since 1913, all due to excessive creation of new money (expansion of the money supply; monetary inflation). This hurts the people (especially those on limited or fixed incomes, and those with savings), but the bankers have done well, since they make money selling US debt (T-bills, etc.) and get bailed-out when in trouble due to their own greed (Bear-Stearns in 2008, etc.). Most Fed meetings are secret, and proceedings are not even available to Congress; Preposterous ! Some economists say the Fed is needed in order to assure adequate 'liquidity' or 'elasticity' for growth by proper expansion of the money supply, equal to growth of the economy; about 3 to 5% per year. The problem is that such powers are **ALWAYS** abused by governments (by expansion of 10 to 20% per year, or more!), though some (the Swiss) less than others (the US is among the worst of the major currencies). **We cannot, and should not, trust the government or Fed to 'manage' our monetary system**. This excess money causes bad spending and investment decisions at both the business and personal level, which creates financial distortions (big peaks, then valleys), as seen in: 1. Bailing-out England after WW1, leading to mal-investment (too much money around) and the crash of 1929 when, after ten years of excessive expansion, the money supply was suddenly reduced by about 30% by the Fed, and 2. The 2007-2008 housing price and construction collapse due to a Fed interest rate increase of 4.25% (from 1 to 5.25%) in 2006, and 3. Many other large peaks and valleys, and 90% loss of purchasing value, since the Fed was created. So much for government 'management' of currency and the economy!!

As James Quinn wrote on his web site www.The BurningPlatform.com, in his article 'Grand Illusion – The Federal Reserve': *"The average American might just conclude that prices always go up, so what's the big deal about inflation. This is where the Federal Reserve and politicians have pulled the wool over your eyes. The CPI was 30.9 in 1964. Today, it is 211.1. This means that prices have risen 683% since 1964. The only problem is that your wages have not risen at the same rate, even using the government manipulated CPI. Using a true CPI figure, average weekly earnings are 64% below what they were in 1964. This explains why a family of five could live well with one parent working in 1964, but even with both parents working and using debt in prodigious amounts, the average family does not live as well today."*

When nations used real money (gold coins, and tokens and certificates redeemable for gold), they had small highs and lows in their economies, but they were 'self-liquidating' (private investors stop putting limited funds into bad deals), and they never had the huge variations now caused by excessive fake money (investors and the government have lots of money to keep funding lots of deals; good and bad).

The analogy below helps demonstrate what fake money does to an economy, its firms, and people.

The Heroin Analogy

The injection of heroin into your body, or a large increase in the money supply (over 5% per year) into an economy, are both 'stimulants', but cause illness when used to excess. When the stimulants are ended to solve the bad effects, your body suffers from withdrawal, and the economy from recession, or worse! Creating fake money to fund 'stimulus' risks price inflation (reduced purchasing power of the US dollar), but or 'leaders' in DC like it because it is a quick 'fix' (shows that they are 'doing something'), and also helps them payoff their friends (campaign donors) on Wall Street, and federal debt, with cheap dollars. This is part of the heroin analogy, where our 'leaders' (Obama, Geithner, Bush, Paulson, and most Congresspersons) are shameless, dishonest pushers and dealers with their 'bailout' programs. Their priority is to get re-elected (or keep their appointed job) by doing favors for voters, their bosses, and campaign donors, no matter what the long-term harm to the nation and its people!

Global investor Jim Rogers (JimRogers.com) said in Nov-2010; "**The banks who lent the money and made the mistakes should lose money. The bondholders and the**

stockholders of those banks should lose money. It's that simple." The logic applies equally in the USA, but campaign donors and pals got bailed-out instead.

As shown in the May 5, 2009 issues of Gary North's Reality Check, Issue 854, www.GaryNorth.com, *"The FED is engaged in a gigantic system of misrepresentation. It is misrepresenting the solvency of large banks and financial firms in debt to banks.The FED is doing its best to conceal the degree of risk and uncertainty in the capital markets. Central banks around the world are cooperating with the FED. This is an international effort by central bankers to deceive the public. To the extent that this deception is working, investor confidence will increase.*

On April 15, 2008, the FED held $866 billion in assets, which served as the monetary base for the nation. On April 15, 2009, it held $2.2 trillion! "

These increases are the same as giving more heroin to a sick addict. See more on inflation below.

Some say the Fed should be eliminated because it is a preposterous, damaging, and unconstitutional scheme. Others prefer to just reform it (audits, transparency, etc.). I am in the former camp, and add that we should convert to gold money as discussed in Chapter 4. If we convert to the gold standard, the world will soon follow as fake money is refused by Sellers; a reverse form of; a) Gresham's Law (without legal tender laws), and b) Nixon's cut of the dollar's tie to gold in 1971. In this case, good money drives out bad. This would end the justification by all governments for money control and manipulation groups such as central banks worldwide, the BIS, World Bank, IMF, FDIC, legal tender laws, etc., all of which should be abolished.

Bernanke and his pals worldwide would need to look for useful, productive, honest work. Good riddance!
 The above heroin analogy sends the message that you will always get counter-productive conduct when you flood a system (nation, industry, family) with money. Examples are:

1. Student Loans: Student loans and Pell Grants (no repayment) seem like a 'nice' thing for governments to provide, but they have resulted in the annual cost of attending college (tuition, books, fees, housing, and meals) in the 1960s going up over twice as fast as starting salaries for graduates. This is due to higher teacher and administrator salaries, more teachers (often with a low teaching load) and support staff, excessive building construction, the growing inefficiency of tenure, etc. 'Hot' professors get raises due to bidding wars between schools that want them. GROWTH is a top goal for most college presidents! These expenses are fed by an unending supply of money from students. The college 'industry' is the only one that can keep raising prices without losing customers (students); they just borrow more! Student loan debt now exceeds credit card debt! ($1,025 vs $843 bn,; 22% more!)

2. Government Payments: Health care costs have soared since Medicare started in the 1960's. When it costs them little or nothing, patients don't care what a service costs, or if excessive services are used.

Econ 101 says we should expect price increases in any industry (college and health above, or any other) where the firms and customers can get money from the government at special rates or free, and there is little connection to 'return on investment'! It's an old story of unsustainable distortions caused by government meddling with the economy (social-engineering, stimulants, depressants, controls, etc., etc.). This also causes price inflation (reduced purchasing power of the Dollar), but government people like monetary inflation because they have more money to pay off their debts, though the creditor gets less-valuable paper. Again, this is a form of partial default.

The solution is to use real money and free markets so there is a stable supply of money, and 1. Thus not enough funding for wars and other corrupt deals, and 2. Failing deals aren't funded for long (with fiat money, government deals usually get MORE money when in trouble!). Not perfect, but many times better results (peace, prosperity, justice, etc.) than produced by government 'management' and meddling (intervention in the free market)!

Monopoly Money and Legal Tender Laws

I remember being asked sometime in about 1995 whether I thought Greenspan was doing a good job. I replied that 'It's not a matter of who has the job, I don't want the Fed to exist!' The Fed tends to increase the money supply too much in an effort to 'stimulate' the economy. Congressional 'leaders' like Sen. Dodd and Rep. Frank, and others, kept asking for more! Only a few people in Congress (Senators Hagel, McCain, Dole and others, and Rep. Paul) raised the red flag in the 2000 to 2005 period about the risks of excessive money creation, but they were ignored. The crash of Oct-2008 was the result!

The Fed measures the quantity of U.S. money ('money supply') worldwide in four ways, in order of liquidity (how close it is to cash): M0= basic money supply (Fed Notes and coins = currency, cash), M1 = M0 + checking account deposits, M2 = M1 + near-money (savings accounts, mutual funds, etc; quick conversion to money), and M3 = M2 + large time-deposits (over $100k). They stopped publishing M3 in 2006 claiming high costs, but do they actually have something to hide? Private sources estimated M3 at $14 trillion in mid 2010, of which $6 trill. was overseas. Less than ten percent of M1 is coins or paper (= 'currency'). The rest is only in electronic form on computers.

But there is another part of the money supply, namely unused credit (credit 'lines'). As John Mauldin, of www.frontlinethoughts.com, penned on April 17, 2009: " *It's a bit misleading to talk about money supply, because money really is roughly $2 trillion of cash and then $50 trillion in credit. Because what do the banks do? They take deposits in and then they borrow money to leverage them up (this is their deal with the Fed: maintain about ten percent 'reserves', the actual deposits, and then borrow your 'lending money' from the Fed). I take my credit card and I spend with it. I borrow against a house. I have an asset that rises, and I borrow against it.*

We have $2 trillion of actual cash propping up $50 trillion in credit. If we all decided to settle and pay off everything, we couldn't do it because there is not enough cash. There would be massive asset deflation. We, as a nation, are leveraged 25 to 1, or we were. Now, that $50 trillion is in a real sense the money supply because that is what we are all pretending is real money. I lend you money and you pretend you are going to pay me back. Then you pretend he is not going to call your debt for cash, and we are all going to keep the system going. "

In addition to creating the Fed, the government tampers with money in other ways, such as **'Legal Tender' laws.** Early controls, such as Art.1, Sec. 10 of the Constitution shown below, were used to assure that only 'real' commodity-based money was produced by the government, but politicians find ways to avoid these limits. Ignoring the Constitution is a convenient method, and no one seems to mind! Later, laws were designed to force people to accept fake money, such as Civil War 'Greenbacks', rather than insist on gold, etc. This forced

Sellers to accept government money when offered (tendered) if they wanted legal recognition of deals (i.e., enforceable in court). These laws are usually a sign of weakness and fraud in a monetary system. Primary U.S. monetary laws are now as follows:

"The U.S. Constitution, Art. I Sec. 10 Cl. 1, states, in part: 'No State shall ... coin Money; emit Bills of Credit; make any Thing but gold and silver Coin a Tender in Payment of Debts; ...'.

During the early American Civil War, the federal government first issued United States Demand Notes (the first 'greenback' notes). They were redeemable in gold and silver coin, and became in shortage due to hoarding. Due to eventual difficulties in redeeming Demand Notes (lack of gold in mint reserves), a money-strapped Congress which had to pay for the war, adopted the Legal Tender Act of 1862, thus compelling people to accept these United States Notes, backed only by treasury securities, as payment for debts. Once forced to accept federal banknotes, the recipients wanted to be able to use them to pay their own debts to each other, and this led to litigation from those who did not want to accept them, but instead preferred coin. The United States Supreme Court ruled the practice unconstitutional in Hepburn v. Griswold in 1870, but later reversed this decision following the appointment of two new judges by President Ulysses S Grant. The Court held that paper money, even that not backed by specie such as the United States Notes, can be legal tender, in the Legal Tender Cases, ranging from 1871 to 1884.
On the other hand, coins made of gold or silver may not necessarily be legal tender, if they are not fiat money in the jurisdiction where they are preferred as payment. The United States Coinage Act of 1965 states (in part);

*'United States coins and currency (including
Federal Reserve notes and circulating notes
of Federal reserve banks and national banks)
are legal tender for all debts, public charges,
taxes and dues. Foreign gold or silver coins
are not legal tender for debts.'*

*Title 31 of the US Code outlines the role of legal tender.
Foreign gold or silver coins are not legal tender for debts. '
This statute means that all United States money as
identified above are a valid and legal offer of payment for
debts when tendered to a creditor in the U.S.." (from
www.wikipedia.org)*

Another example of serious tampering is when FDR issued
the Gold Recall Act (illegal Executive Order 6102) in 1933
that made it illegal for US citizens to own gold anywhere in
the world, except for jewelry, and rare coins. This was
codified by the Gold Reserve Act of 1934. It demonetized
gold, and increased the government holdings. There are
two explanations for this action:
1. The 'official' reason is that FDR was worried because
foreign nations were redeeming their paper USD to gold
because they knew the U.S. was running out of it. That was
true, but it was only part of the plan. To replenish the
government supply the people were forced to sell it to the
government in exchange for the going rate of $20.67 of
paper Fed Notes per ounce. But after he had the gold, he
increased the 'official' price to $35 oz ! (a bonus for the
government !). The Act also voided contracts, and
prohibited new ones, that called for settlement in gold (a
'gold clause').These restrictions on gold ownership were
weakened over the years, and ended in 1975.
2. The 'true' reason is that FDR wanted to create new
money to pay for his planned New Deal programs so used
the above confiscation and restrictions as a tricky way to
end the right of gold redemption by citizens concerned

43

about such inflation. Now he could create all the money he wanted!

The Act also established the Exchange Stabilization Fund (ESF), which is still active. Initially funded by the above 'bonus' from gold confiscation, it had assets of $51.2 bill. as of June-2008. Its function is to use this special fund to: a. purchase or sell foreign currencies (manipulate the market!), b. hold U.S. foreign exchange and IMF-created 'Special Drawing Rights' (SDR) assets, and c. to provide financing to foreign governments (p. 71, Mexico), all aimed at bringing stability to the foreign exchange market (read, 'manipulate it to suit the US'). There is strong evidence that it was used in the 1990s to intervene (i.e., sell US gold) in the public gold market to suppress the price of gold (a high gold price makes fiat money look bad), and again in 2011 and 2012 (took gold from $1,900 oz. to $1,500). The Sec. of the Treasury has broad discretion in use of the money, and only his signature is required, and the transactions are not made known, even to Congress. We need to audit the Fed to reveal how much gold they still have, and of what quality.

In Jan-2013 Germany asked for return the 300 tonnes of gold it had stored in the Fed vault in New York (some say they were annoyed by the above secret price meddling in 2011). It is scheduled to be complete by 2020; 7 years! Why so long? In earlier attempts to verify the existence of its gold, the Fed only allowed Germans to take a peek into the vault, but no audit. Is it there, or has it been used for ESF dealing, leased, etc.?? If the Fed has to buy gold in the market to restore the German gold, it could cause a 'repatriation run' if the world (nations, banks and people) decide they want to possess their gold. For example, delivery requests on the COMEX for physical gold are usually about 10 tonnes per month, but for Feb-2013 are reaching 43 tons!

While the1933 confiscation of gold effectively ended redeemability of paper 'money' for gold by mere people, the 1944 **'Bretton Woods Agreement'** made it formal. This deal is named for the resort area in NH where major nations met to arrange world money 'management' in July, 1944. They set rules to: 1. Allow only nations to redeem paper for gold between each other (not people; a form of the Gold Bullion Exchange standard), 2. Create the International Monetary Fund (IMF; www.imf.org) to handle its foreign exchange transactions, and promote 'stability and cooperation' between nations (also used to payoff bank loans, then impose 'austerity' to make the people repay the IMF!), 3. Create the World Bank (www.worldbank.org; 1 of 5 orgs in this group) to make loans to developing nations to reduce poverty (or bribe dictators, and 4**. Set the USD as the 'official' (not determined by market usage) world's reserve currency**, with a fixed value of $35 per ounce of gold. In 1961 the U.S. and seven Euro countries created the 'London Gold Pool' to buy and sell gold to stabilize prices. It failed in 1968. The U.S. engaged in so much monetary expansion (inflation of the money supply) after WW2 (VietNam, Medicare, welfare) it lost much of its value and due to high spending there, flooded Europe with so-called 'Euro-dollars'. France finally started demanding gold for most of their paper dollars, which peaked with De Gaulle's famous press conference on Feb. 4, 1965 where he described the U.S. as having an 'exorbitant privilege' as the world's reserve currency, which allowed us to pay our debts with money created out of thin air. France started redeeming their paper dollars to gold, but Nixon soon refused to remit gold to any nation (we were running out), and then abrogated Bretton Woods on Aug. 15, 1971, setting the dollar 'afloat' with no redeemability. Soon, all nations had done the same, including conservative Switzerland, and everybody could make money out of thin air! Great job security for Central Bank 'meddling-managers'!

Figure 1: Monetary Base (M0) 1918 to 2011

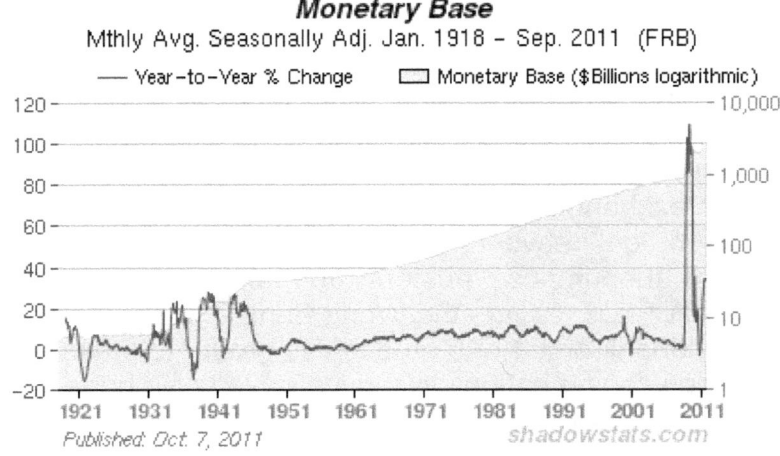

Figure 1 shows how the US money supply increased rapidly after 1971 (Nixon ended the tie to gold) and then spiked with Fed Chm. Bernanke's 'Quantitative Easing' (create new money) in 2008.

Analysis of Figure 1: The Federal Reserve System started in 1913, helped fund WW1, did large M0 increase in early 1920s to help England after WW1, then reduced M0 quickly due to market frenzy in mid '20s, a major cause of the 1929 depression. The Fed increased M0 to fund WW2, and increased it in the '80s as a stimulant after '80-81 recession, which led to the 'dot.com bubble' in '90s. Interest rates were reduced in 2000 to 2006 to boost housing and recover from the dot.com bubble crash in March-2000. 'Easy money' became the underlying cause of the 2002-7 housing bubble, then its burst, as this money fed the CRA, Fannie, Freddie, Main Street, and Wall Street binges of excessive spending, debt, and fraud! The

'Bernanke Spike' of $2 trill. in late 2008 was to stimulate the economy after the housing bubble burst in 2007. It didn't work. Constant meddling fails !

****

The Fed destroys the value of our money by excessive expansion of the money supply ('monetary inflation') and other meddling. Proof is shown in the start and end "purchase power" amounts below, which are from www.measuringworth.com:

1774 to 1912: It took $1,202.05 in the year 1912 for the same "purchase power" as $1,000 in the year 1774 (a 17.7% loss in 138 yrs, or 0.13 % per yr).

1913 to 2008: It took $22,427.40 in the year 2008 for the same "purchase power" as $1,000 in the year 1913 (a 95.5% loss in 95 yrs, or 1.0% per yr). Almost eight times worse than before the Fed!

2009 thru 2014: The US Federal Reserve held between $700 billion and $800 billion of Treasury notes on its balance sheet before the recession. In late November 2008, the Fed started buying $600 billion in Mortgage-backed securities (MBS). By March 2009, it held $1.75 trillion of bank debt, MBS, and Treasury notes, and reached a peak of $2.1 trillion in June 2010. Further purchases were halted as the economy had started to improve, but resumed in August 2010 when the Fed decided the economy wasn't growing enough and bought $30 billion in 2–10 year Treasury notes a month. In November 2010, the Fed announced a second round of quantitative easing, or "QE2", buying $600 billion of Treasury securities by the end of the second quarter of 2011. Since late 2013 they have 'tapered' to smaller buys and the program as of June, 2014 stands at $45 billion per month. Fed Chairman Janet Yellen expects the program to wind down steadily through 2014 and conclude by year-end, assuming the economy remains healthy! (Ha! What 'health') The Fed admitted loaning almost $3 tn to European banks, along with large loans to US banks and businesses (especially those with good political connections). All this was done secretly with no Congressional oversight. No wonder there is a movement to 'End the Fed'.

The above favors to businesses end up as a hidden 'inflation tax' on US citizens. A decline in purchasing power of the dollar, and thus price increases, always follows a rapid and excessive (over 5% per year) increase in the money supply (monetary inflation). As shown in Figure 2 below, the dollar lost 95% of its value from 1913 (when the Fed started) to 2000, but the largest percentage increases in the money supply occurred after Nixon cut the Bretton Woods tie to gold in 1971. Other factors, such as a reduced supply of goods and services, can cause price increases, but monetary inflation has caused the most harm (See Figure 1 above). An example of distorting the supply of consumer goods is the payroll for workers in aerospace and military industries, where the workers have more money, but the things they produce are not available for purchase.

Figure 2
Purchasing Power of the US Dollar

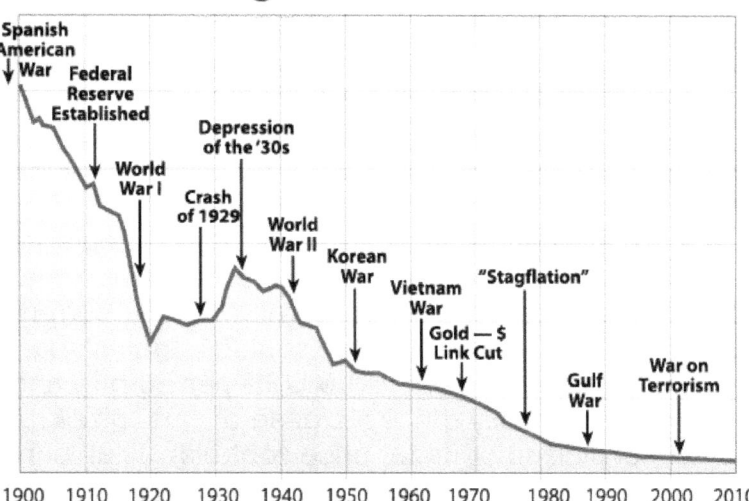

The Incredible Shrinking Dollar — Down 95%

When dollars only buy 5% of what they used to, even having $1 million hardly counts as 'rich' anymore.

Source: Byron King, www.agorafinancial.com

The US dollar has lost over 95% of its purchasing power since 1913 due to excessive monetary inflation by the Fed (creating new money for the government to pay bills). This has been the main cause of the 2,000 % increase (20X) in price inflation since 1913. Excessive money creation by banks prior to 1913 resulted in short-term inflation and 'panics' (runs on insolvent banks), but after 1913 the Fed allowed long-term abuse by bailing-out such banks, which in turn caused the 'moral hazard' (taking high risks with the expectation of a bailout if needed) of the banks taking excessive risks by seeking 'casino' profits since the early 1990s.

Internationally, the USD emerged as the world's reserve currency (good as gold) after WW1 because all fiat paper money (not redeemable for a commodity) is actually viewed as a share in the economy of the issuer. Thus, the paper of a large and stable government and economy has good value (the best choice within the world's fake money). Until 2008 the US was without question the world's strongest economy, and thus the USD had good value as a 'share' (like 'stock') in 'USA, Inc.'. Since 1971, the US has abused its currency by inflating its supply even more than other countries, borrowed and spent to excess, and the dollars' value has decreased (prices increased) rapidly ever since (look at any chart) on both the international exchange basis (about 4:1 against western Europe 'legacy' currencies from 1971 to 1999, then a loss of about 2:1 against the Euro from 1999 to 2008; 0.8 to 1.5 USD per Euro !), and by about 10:1 domestically (price increase of cars, pizza, etc.; things not subsidized or under price controls). Thus our 'share of USA Inc.' money is decreasing in value and confidence as viewed by other nations, and they are seeking less dependency on the USD as the primary reserve currency for the world. This has massive implications on our ability to create new money to pay our bills to other countries, and could result in a crash (loss of 50% or more of purchasing power) of the USD!!

Central Banking and Meddling Worldwide

The various central banks worldwide, and the parasitic politicians, staff, and bailout recipients who feed off them, are another layer of monetary manipulation and damage. With a self-regulating (if allowed) gold standard, they would all be looking for useful, honest work. Good!

Major organizations are:

A. Bank for International Settlements (BIS): The BIS, established by the Hague agreements of 1930 to handle German debt from WW1, is an international organization of 55 central banks, based in Basel, Switzerland. It claims to *"foster international monetary and financial cooperation and serves as a bank for central banks"* , and says it seeks to make monetary policy more predictable and transparent among its member central banks. Although a private corporation, the BIS, its offices, employees, directors and members share an incredible immunity from virtually all regulation, scrutiny and accountability, with quasi diplomatic status granted and supported by the Swiss government. Many believe the BIS is; 1. Controlled by elite bankers to serve not just the interests of their nation, but also of business and personal 'friends', and 2. Is the cause of most currency-related problems. Stay tuned!

B. The Central Bank Gold Agreement (CBGA): Also known as the 'Washington Agreement on Gold', it was announced on September 26, 1999. It followed a period of increasing concern that uncoordinated central bank gold sales were destabilising the market, driving the gold price sharply down. (http://www.gold.org/government_affairs/)

Central banks held around 33,000 tonnes of gold in September 1999 (then to 30,563 in 2011), nearly a quarter of all the gold estimated to be above ground, so their actions were of key interest to the gold market.

Much of this interest focused on the central banks of Western Europe. Many of these held - and still hold - substantial stocks of gold in their reserves. Some (Netherlands, Belgium, Austria, Switzerland and the UK) figured among those banks which had recently sold gold or announced plans to do so. At the same time, with rising demand for borrowed gold, a number of central banks were increasing their use of lending, swaps and other gold derivative instruments (hence the need for audits; see ESF on page 45). Due to the workings of the gold derivatives market, an increase in gold lending normally results in additional gold being sold. That's why this growth in lending was adding to the amount of gold supplied to the market.

In addition to the destabilizing effect of these sales, market fears about central bank intentions were causing further falls in the price of gold. The market falls caused considerable pain for gold producing countries.

In response to these concerns, fifteen European central banks (those of the then 11 Eurozone countries plus the European Central Bank and those of non-member Sweden, Switzerland and the UK) drew up the first Central Bank Gold Agreement in 1999. A far better plan would have been to trash the fake Euro, and convert all the nations to the Gold Standard! The Euro crisis, ongoing since early 2011, confirms this.

C. Elite Private Groups: 1) 'The Bilderberg Group': This is a private club for 'world leaders'. The original Bilderberg conference (bilderberg.org, or bilderbergmeetings.org) was held at the Hotel de Bilderberg in the Netherlands in1954. Its focus is on world monetary affairs and holds an annual invitation-only conference for persons of influence in the fields of politics, business, and banking to talk about a variety of global issues, **2) 'World Economic Forum':** Davos. Switzerland has hosted the WEF (weforum.org) since 1988. It is an annual meeting of global political and business elites to discuss world problems and solutions, **3) 'The Trilateral Commission'** (trilateral.org) was created in 1973 to bring together experienced leaders within the private sector to discuss issues of global concern at a time when communication and cooperation between Europe, North America, and Asia were lacking, **4)** The **'Council on Foreign Relations'** (cfr.org) is an American nonprofit, publisher and think tank specializing in U.S. foreign policy and international affairs. It was founded in 1921, and **5)** Founded as a scholarly group in 1947, the **Mont Pelerin Society** (www.montpelerin.org) meets annually in places worldwide. The society advocates freedom of expression, free market economic policies, and the political values of an open society. **6)** Russia sponsors the annual '**St. Petersburg International Economic Forum',** their answer to Davos. The sixth one was May 22-24, 2014. World business and political leaders are invited to discuss issues, and make buy-sell deals.

D. G-20: This group of 20 major nations (www.G20.org), and the European Community Bank (ECB), started in 1999, and has an annual meeting in a major city (and fancy hotel) to discuss 'money problems'. It evolved from the G-8, which was founded in 1975, as the main economic council of wealthy nations. It became G-7 when Russia was ejected in March, 2014 over the Crimea issue.

The G-20 web site, and press releases after their meetings, make grand statements on how they will save the world's financial system, but they accomplish little because the group has little authority. The meeting in Cannes, France in Oct-2011 is a good example. It was followed by a special meeting there in Nov-2011 to deal with the critical Greek situation (default, leave Euro?) and other problems in the Euro-Zone of seventeen nations (not all are in G20). The European Community Bank (ECB; the Euro-Zone central bank) is running short of funds, so there was much talk of 'mandating' the IMF to print more of its Special Drawing Rights (SDR; an IOU that countries can exchange for cash in major currencies; USD, Yen, Sterling and Euros; soon Yuan?) so nations can use them to strengthen their central banks reserves, and allow more borrowing.

The Oct-2011 Group of 20 meeting did nothing to solve the euro crisis, but the (ultimately rejected) suggestion that Germany put up its gold to back up a bailout fund confirmed that gold is once again going to become an important part of the world monetary system.
Russia assumed the G20 presidency for the first time on December 1, 2012. The G20 Leaders' Summit, held in St. Petersburg, Russia, on September 5-6, 2013, was the main G20 event of 2013.

****

The vision of the BIS, CBAG, Bilderberg Group, and G20 for world prosperity (under their control) will fail because it is based on fiat money that has no commodity-based market value, is subject to excessive creation of new money, meddling in the market by self-serving (builds power, income, career security, and vanity) banksters and politicians, and thus unsustainable. The members and guests of these groups love to pontificate about 'problems' and how they will solve them; always with more government intervention. They fear the free market, where high-risk deals, or incompetent and corrupt owners and managers, are allowed to fail (and their investors or depositors lose), and better players take their place. They prefer the perverse incentive of bailouts (central banks admit they are 'lender of last resort') where they can play for high risk-reward deals and never lose! With nations, central banks, and the IMF providing the bailout funds, the bad deals and firms are propped-up and the citizens pay in the form of national debt or price inflation.

All empires fail in part due to running out of purchasing power when their fake money becomes almost worthless. The failed empires of Rome, Italy, Spain, France, England, USSR, etc. are examples. Another sign of failing is decadence of the citizens. Look at how the content of TV, movies, and magazines have changed since the '50s, with

54

more sex, violence and cursing. Just as Romans wanted bread and circuses, with lions and gladiators, our people thrive on the violence of NASCAR and cheating and fighting in sports, or the silliness of 'Dancing with the Stars'.

Starting in the late '90s, Pres. Clinton and Rep. Barney Frank (the worst mortgage abusers) pushed Fannie and Freddie to 'help the poor' (and vote for me) by making more subprime loans, many of which were then sold to Wall Street to be securitized. As Peter Schiff (www.peter-schiff.com) wrote on Feb. 14, 2009; *"Developed primarily over the last 10 years, securitization permitted loans of all shapes and sizes to be packaged into investment-ready securities. The system worked, fueling unprecedented levels of lending in the home, auto, student, and credit card sectors. But in the last few years, as the collateral underpinning of these securities has collapsed in value, the trillions of dollars of securitized debt now in circulation has become the toxic sludge at the bottom of our financial pit."*

Foreign banks and investors happily bought trillions of dollars of these securities because they were primarily based on US real estate, had high interest income, and were apparently backed by the US government. The process was corrupt from the start, but was pushed by Congress and Wall Street elites. As the false prosperity slowed, and caused loss of US jobs, then mortgage foreclosures, these fake securities lost value, and the worldwide crash started in late 2008.

Euro Woes
From the beginning of the Greek debt crisis in April 2010, the Greek bailout has been about saving the Western banks that had purchased the Greek government's IOUs. The member states must be provided with euros, so that they can continue to make interest payments to the banks. Mario Draghi, an Italian banker and economist, succeeded

Jean-Claude Trichet as the President of the European Central Bank (ECB) on 1 November 2011. He is expected to be aggressive in centralizing financial planning in the Eurozone (bye, bye, sovereignty!). The British BREXIT vote occurred on June 23, 2016 and showed voter preference to leave the EU. It caused an uproar in markets, and prompted talk of other nations leaving (France, Germany, Greece, Spain?).

The northern nations were using the **European Financial Stability Facility** (EFSB) to support the south (Portugal, Italy, Greece, Spain; the PIGS), but this proved insufficient to control the panic. Another bailout facility, the **European Stability Mechanism (ESM),** was finally approved by Germany's courts in Sep-2012 that is much bigger and more permanent. It is as a €700bn fund that includes the €80bn of capital that is being provided by euro countries, plus €620bn of guarantees. It will have a lending capacity of €500bn, all run by the ECB. Ben Bernanke secretly gave (loaned?) the ECB trillions of USD to bail them out, and thus avoid damage to the USD. This was preposterous and should be illegal! Since early 2012, the Euro and USD have bounced-around in value as the world made choices of the 'least bad' currency.

Another disaster struck on March 17, 2013 when the Eurozone announced a €10 bn 'bail-in' of major Cyprus banks, that would be paid for by a 'tax' on deposits. Then on April 28, 2013, Bank of Cyprus, the island's largest bank, said; 1) It had converted 37.5 % of deposits over 100,000 euros into "class A" shares, with 22.5 % held as a buffer for possible conversion in the future, and 2) 30 % would be 'temporarily' frozen and held as deposits. That leaves only 10% available to the 'owners'!

Surprise, any government can do whatever they want, despite prior agreements and laws. Get used to it! They have the guns and courts. I say the worldwide central bank efforts to make these and other fiat currencies work are doomed, and should be, because they exist (despite PR and Lies to the contrary) only to serve banksters and politicians. Many U.S. banks are exposed to the Eurozone problems, and could be hurt; We'll see.

Will Germany end the futile game by reviving a gold-backed 'New Deutsche Mark'? They need to break-loose from the Euro mess, as Ludwig Erhard did in 1948 when he ended post-war price controls and the Germany economy blossomed. To see my essays on this, and other monetary topics, go to my archive at ActivistPost.com, scroll to bottom of Home page and select 'Contributors', then my name.

Avoiding the U.S. Dollar

The trend is to use less of the USD as a 'reserve currency' for international transactions. This will; 1. Reduce demand for dollars, and result in a major (50 to 80% ?) drop in value, and 2. Limit the USA's ability to get USD denominated loans at low rates (by selling bonds), and then repay them with newly created dollars; DeGaulle called it our **Exorbitant Privilege!**

Countries we buy imports from (China leads) accumulate billions of USD and buy our T-bills to get some interest (and help feed future purchases by the U.S.?). This is a re-cycling of fake money, with interest paid by fake money, with all parties hoping it will last forever! Foreign nations that hold large amounts of USD-denominated assets (mostly bonds) are getting nervous that the USD will drop in value, so they are looking for ways to avoid dependency on, and ownership of, USDs. A flight to safety is starting, and could lead to a collapse in USD value. Fake money requires demand to keep its PP. Gold is safe, and this why the Russian central bank has added 570 metric tons of the metal in the past decade, a quarter more than runner-up China, according to IMF data. Based on these gold purchases, maybe China and Russia are planning to destroy the petrodollar system by using gold as money, and thus crash the U.S. economy by ending the USD's role as a reserve currency? (see P.20)

The BRICS: The BRICS are Brazil, Russia, India, China, and South Africa. They started trading with each other in their own currencies in 2011, thus reducing demand for the USD, and speeding its fall in value! If we keep spending and borrowing too much, and keep creating new money to pay for it; 1) The USD will crash in purchasing power (PP), 2) The price of foreign purchases will rise, and 3) Interest rates will soar for our debt. When this occurs we will pay existing foreign debts and interest with our near-worthless paper money. This is debt default by hyperinflation. No country wants this to happen, especially our creditors and holders of cash and USD denominated assets. Thus they discuss alternatives for a smooth departure from the current dependency on the USD and banking system for world trade. A major step was taken at the sixth summit of the BRICS in Brazil on July 15-17, 2014 when they set up:1) the $100 billion '**New Development Bank**' and, 2) a reserve currency fund worth $100 billion. Each country has a different share.

Africa and Mideast: Gadhaffi was pushing use of the gold Dinar for all sales of oil by African nations. This, along with evicting the 35,000 Chinese workers in Libya, and controlling their oil, was the real reason we and NATO invaded in Apr-2011. Part of Saddam Hussein's death warrant was to convert Iraq oil sales to payment in Euros in 2002. China and Russia suggested at the Jan-2009 'World Economic Forum' in Davos that a new system is needed to replace the USD as the world's primary reserve currency, then they agreed to trade in their own currencies. In Aug-2011, China and France agreed to form a task force to discuss how the Yuan could become part of the SDR. It is said they want 20% USD (was 42%), 20% Yuan, 20% Yen, 20% Euro, and 20% Pound Sterling. In Dec-2011 China and Japan agreed to trade in their own currencies. In Jan-2012 Iran said it would sell oil to India in Rupees. China holds trillions of USD denominated bonds and other assets, and doesn't want the USD to crash. Is this why in Feb-2013, China's central bankers suggest the world is moving "to a '1+4' system, with the greenback serving as the anchor of global payments, supplemented by 'four smaller reserve currencies' – the euro, sterling, yen and yuan." In any combination of the above trends, the USD is sliding from its mighty perch!

Even the solid Swiss Franc is under pressure. In Sep-2011 the Swiss National Bank (their central bank) announced they would buy Euros 'as needed' to reduce the strength of the Swiss Franc which had been hurting exports. Thomas Jacob, a monetary activist in Zurich, has started http://www.goldfranc.org/ to seek parliamentary approval to issue a Swiss coin containing gold. Good luck Thomas!

China Seeks Power: China made a major announcement on Oct. 24, 2014 with the creation the **Asian Infrastructure Investment Bank (AiiBank.org)**, a multilateral development bank to provide finance to infrastructure projects in the Asia region. AIIB is regarded by some as a rival for the IMF, the World Bank and the Asian Development Bank (ADB), which are dominated by developed countries like the United States. As of April 15, 2015, almost all Asian countries and most major countries outside Asia (total of 50) had joined the AIIB, except the US, Japan (which dominated the ADB) and Canada. North Korea's and Taiwan's applications for

59

Prospective Founding Member (PFM) were rejected. The rush of our 'friends' in Europe to join is an indication of China's growing economic power. It is not clear which currency the AIIB will use. It could be the Yuan, or even the IMF SDR, with the Yuan included. Either choice would reduce the USD dominance as a reserve currency, an ominous step toward collapse of the US economy!! On Aug. 4, 2015 the IMF announced the above SDR changes would **NOT** occur at the IMF annual meeting to be held in Lima, Peru in Oct-2015! This rejection was pushed by the U.S. based on the fact that China's debt is 280% of their GDP, thus too weak to be part of the SDR. Then on Nov. 13, 2015, IMF chief Christine Lagarde said the fund now deemed the yuan "meets the requirements to be a 'freely usable' currency" -- a key hurdle to joining the yen, dollar, pound, and euro as a leading unit in international trade. This implied the yuan (same as 'Renminbi') could be formally admitted to the IMF's "special drawing rights" currency basket at the IMFs' Nov. 30, 2015 meeting in Sweden. Indeed! On Monday, Nov. 30, the IMF announced their approval of the Chinese renminbi as one of the world's main central bank reserve currencies, and part of the SDR. Minor changes in the percent of each currency in the SDR left the USA at 42, China now 11, and reductions for Yen to 8, Euro to 31, and the UK pound to 8. The changes will take effect in Oct-2016.

The IMF decision will help pave the way for broader use of the renminbi in trade and finance, securing China's standing as a global economic power. Chinese leaders view it as a giant step up for their place in world economics! The trouble is that much of the increase in demand for the yuan/renminbi will reduce demand for the USD, and its' purchasing power will fall even faster. Peter Schiff (SchiffGold.com) said; 'Another issue is a possible Chinese move to un-peg the yuan from the dollar, which could set off a worldwide economic earthquake.

Chapter 3:
The US Banking and Securities System

The System includes,

1. 'Commercial Banks', which provide checking, loan, and other services, and accept customer deposits. Some are state chartered, and others are chartered and supervised by the OCC and use the word 'national' in their name.
2. 'Investment Banks' which invest their own, and shareholders, capital in securities, mortgages, etc. (not securities brokers or dealers), and with 1999 changes in the 1933 Glass-Stegall started accepting customer deposits (which led to the abuses that crashed in 2008!),
3. 'Savings and Loan Institutions' ('Thrifts'), which provide home mortgages, and accept customer deposits, and
4. 'Stock Exchanges' (SE), which sell securities (shares) issued by corporations. Examples are: New York SE, Pacific SE, NASDAQ, etc.

The 'system' is regulated by the:
1. 'Federal Reserve System'
2. 'Securities and Exchange Commission' (SEC), created in 1934 to regulate securities markets,
3. 'Federal Deposit Insurance Corp.' (FDIC) which insures deposits up to $250,000 against bank failures,
4. 'Office of Comptroller of Currency' (OCC) was started in 1863 as a bureau of the U.S. Department of the Treasury. The OCC's main purpose was to create federally chartered national banks that could issue 'Treasury Notes', and tax (thus end) issuance of money by state banks, and create a Federal monopoly. (more on P. 18)
5. 'Commodity Futures Trading Commission' (CFTC) is an independent agency of the US government. Its mission is to protect market users and the public from fraud, manipulation, and abusive practices related to the sale of commodity and financial futures and options, and to foster

open, competitive, and financially sound futures and option markets,

6. 'Office of Thrift Supervision' (OTS), an agency of the United States Department of the Treasury, is the primary regulator of federal savings associations (sometimes referred to as federal thrifts). Federal savings associations include both federal savings banks and federal savings and loans. The OTS is also responsible for supervising savings and loan holding companies (SLHCs) and some state-chartered institutions. The OTS was established by Congress as a bureau of the Department of the Treasury on August 9, 1989 as part of the Financial Institutions Reform, Recovery and Enforcement Act of 1989.

7. 'The Federal Housing Finance Agency' (formed in Sep-2008 as part of the bailout), conservator to regulate Super GSE's FannieMae and FreddieMac. And

8. The 'Troubled Assets Relief Program' (TARP) became the manager of the Oct-2008 $700+ billion bailout of Wall Street and banking firms. The initial plan was to buy toxic mortgage-based assets from Wall Street firms, but by Nov-2008 the target had shifted helping with frozen consumer debt. What is Next in this 'Panic to Patch' ??

Abuse of the System by Banks and Congress

It's bad enough that self-serving politicians and bankers created the Fed to supply money for themselves and their career-enhancing (job saving) projects and wars, but that's only part of how the banks abuse their customers, the people, and the government. They pay off politicians to get laws that accommodate their schemes to increase profits by entering into high reward but risky deals, while protecting themselves from the risk. The casino culture that caused the 2008 crash and ensuing bailouts of Wall Street form a perfect example.

They sell the toxic CRA mandated 'no-doc', 'fake appraisal', 'sub prime' home mortgages to GSEs Fannie and Freddie the same day they make them. This takes the risk and loan funding off their books while they continue to earn fees for 'servicing' the deal by collecting payments, etc. With the prior deals sold, they still have the reserves needed to make new deals. A real profit churn, with the taxpayers at risk via the GSE's.

Prudent bankers are wary of high-risk projects so they won't go insolvent due to project failures. This became 'no problem' when they created the Fed to be 'lender of last resort' to replenish their reserves, even when the 'market' would avoid them. This is called a 'moral hazard' (acting imprudently because you know you will be bailed-out). The same applies to any business or person with good government 'connections'.

The ownership of deposits has been distorted by friendly judges and Congresspersons to give an advantage to the banks. Deposits were originally considered to remain the property of the depositor (a 'bailment'), but courts ruled that since the specific pieces of money could not be identified in the case of losses that the banks were not accountable. Thus deposits became more like loans to the bank that they could use however they wished (loan to others, etc.).

'Fractional reserve' banking is a big part of the problem. When the Fed sets the legal reserve at a typical 10%, banks can loan ten times more than they have. Example: If you deposit $100, they can loan $1,000 (newly created money), and still have your deposit as a 10% reserve. Note that every time a loan is made, or a credit card issued, the money supply increases, and value of all USDs go down.

Another key problem is the Federal Deposit Insurance Corp. (FDIC). This fake 'insurance' (rates not set by market risks; not adequately funded) was created by the government in 1933 so depositors wouldn't get suspicious of fake money and worry enough to withdraw, or avoid making deposits, and now covers $250,000 per depositor per bank. It back-fired in 1991 when the also fake Federal Home Loan Banks ('Savings and Loan' banks) were deregulated in 1990 (as to rates paid to depositors), yet were still insured. White-collar crooks started or bought S&Ls, offered excessive high interest rates to attract deposits, then paid themselves high salaries and bonuses before going bankrupt due to high costs! It was planned that way. A federal taxpayer-funded bailout ensued as yet another unintended consequence of government intervention in the free (honest) market. As the FDIC bailed-out depositors of failed banks in the 2008 crash, they replenished their depleted fund by fees imposed on the well-managed surviving banks. Why should the prudently managed banks be forced to bail-out the greedy casino banksters? Another rip-off! With sound money the FDIC is not needed.

The FHA (Federal Housing Administration), created in 1934, insures lenders against default by homebuyers. This is another distortion of the market that weakens our economy. Sure enough, use of the FHA was broadened in the 2008 home mortgage crisis to bailout home 'owners' who signed-up for loans they couldn't afford, and lenders who knowingly approved their bad or insufficient credit. This is another case of the government pouring good money after bad, rather than liquidating past counterproductive 'help'.

Another counterproductive monetary intervention is the 'Pension Benefit Guaranty Corporation'. It is an independent agency of the federal government that was created to support (bail-out?) private pension plans. How in the world does Congress justify using taxes (or fake money, or under-funded insurance premiums) to bail out private pension plans? Well, it is called 'buying votes' from pensioners. This is what economists call a 'moral hazard' (or perverse incentive), because it allows firms to under-fund their pension plans without penalty; thus more do it. The same applies to 'Federal Disaster Insurance' (passed by Congress in Nov-2007), and 'National Flood Insurance' (NFIP, 1968) which forces all taxpayers to subsidize rates for 'other people' or land developers (including fees tagged-on to home loans, even in areas with extremely low flood risk; such as a small creek nearby !!) so they can get 'affordable' (subsidized) insurance to build (or rebuild) in high risk (flood, hurricane. etc.) areas. All this applies to FEMA, the disastrous Federal organization that is supposed to help us after disasters, which in fact should be treated as State and local issues! This is more counterproductive 'vote getting' with fake money (the States run out of money, but the Federal government doesn't; it is another form of Federal pork)! FEMA should be abolished.

Yet other damaging contrivances (they distort financial markets) are the federally chartered GSE (Government Sponsored Enterprise) corporations.
A. Congress created the first GSE in 1916 with the Farm Credit System;
B. it initiated GSEs in the home finance segment of the economy with the creation of the Federal Home Loan Banks in 1932; and
C. it targeted education when it chartered Sallie Mae in 1972 (SLM Corporation, NYSE: SLM; commonly known as Sallie Mae; originally the Student Loan Marketing Association); it became a fully private institution via legislation in 1995).
D. Federal National Mortgage Association (FMNA, Fannie Mae, was founded in 1938 by FDR, www.fanniemae.com/). Pres. Johnson converted Fannie to a publicly traded corporation, (FNM) in 1968 so it wouldn't be 'on the books'

as part of the US budget deficit caused by the Viet Nam war.
E. Federal Home Loan Mortgage Corp. (Freddie Mac, in 1970, www.freddiemac.com

These fake organizations were created in part to allow banks to issue 30-year fixed-rate home mortgages (sometimes with liberal terms to qualify; such as 'no job, no money') to 'help' make home purchases 'affordable' (with fake, not market-based rates and terms). The problem is that no sane banker would ever guarantee a rate for 30 years! The game is that private banks sell these loans to home buyers, and then re-sell them to Fannie or Freddie the same day (to get rid of such garbage). Both are listed on the NYSE (FNM and FRE), and because their debts were semi-guaranteed by the U.S. Government ('fully' as of Sep-2008), they are able to borrow at low rates. A further deal is that they pay no state or local taxes, and are not required to disclose internal 'problems' as normal banks are. We saw the predictable result of corrupt management policies in Sep-2008 when the US Treasury and Fed invoked the new 'Housing and Economic Recovery Act of 2008' to bail-out (buy?) failing Fannie and Freddie, then set up 'The Federal Housing Finance Agency' (FHFA) to regulate them. A better solution would have been to liquidate them in bankruptcy! They were key originators of the '2008 Crisis' by fraudulently representing their weak loans (poor borrower credit) as prime when they sold them to Wall Street to be securitized. On September 17, 2008, Byron W. King of www.DailyReckoning.com said: *"It used to be that the job of the Federal Reserve was, as former Chairman William McChesney Martin Jr. told it, "to take away the punch bowl just as the party gets going." Now it seems like the Fed is laying a direct pipeline to the distillery to keep everyone loaded."*

A third player, Ginnie Mae (GNMA), Government National Mortgage Association also provides a link between capital markets (the lenders) and the Federal Housing markets. This makes mortgage-backed securities more attractive to investors, such as pension funds and the like. The main difference between this company and Fannie Mae lies in the government backing. While the backing was only perceived in Fannie Mae (until the government 'bought' it on Sep. 7, 2008), it is real in the case of a Ginnie Mae backed security or mortgage since the US Government owns Ginnie. About 95% of all home loans through FHA (Federal Housing Authority) and the VA (Veterans Administration) are backed by GNMA.

These organizations distort our financial system, since at their fake low loan rates, excessive money goes into housing because low wage earners can buy bigger houses. This is nice for politicians who want votes, but is a misallocation of resources in the overall economy! Of course, the Federal Reserve is part of the game with its rate and reserve manipulations. This is what caused the 'subprime' mortgage crash in 2008! Further, the banks 'borrowed-short, and lent-long', which puts the lender at high risk, and no sane banker would do it. BUT, in the US the Fannie-Freddie twins buy these toxic loans from the banks, and take on the risk. Even socialist Canada, while amortizing the principal over 30 years, requires the interest rate to be adjusted 'to market' every five years, and interest is not tax deductible. They have no Fannie or Freddie equivalents to distort the market, and they allow national branch banking to spread risk. Hence, Canada has been doing well since the US economy plunged in 2008. I recommend that the Canadian approach be adopted by the US. Part of the fun in the US is that Mom and Pop borrower get to pay-off their loan with cheap dollars (the USD value declines every year, 10:1 since 1975, and most wages and salaries go up, but only partially compensate).

In 1999 the '**Banking Act of 1933**' (called the 'Glass-Stegall Act'; yes the same Rep. Carter Glass who helped push the Federal Reserve Act through in 1913!), which created the FDIC and separated investment and commercial bank dealings, management, and ownership, was amended by the 'Gramm–Leach–Bliley Act'. This effectively removed the separation that previously existed between investment banking (which issued securities and used their shareholder's money) and commercial banks (which accepted deposits and loaned the depositor's money). The deregulation also removed conflict of interest prohibitions between investment bankers serving as officers of commercial banks. Many view this change as the 'flexibility' that Wall Street banksters used to commit their customer abuse that was a big part of the crash of 2008!

Excessive money (combined with greed) also hurts the 'big guys'. The Mar-2008 bailout of investment bank Bear-Stearns by the Fed (and injection of over $200 bill. 'liquidity' for others) was to prevent the bankruptcy of Bear Stearns, and its ripple effect on others, caused by high-risk, high-leverage (up to 40:1), high-profit investments that got into trouble. The Fed stepped in to save the US 'financial system'. What a pathetic, costly joke! They damage the system with 'loose' money, then try to fix it with more of the same. Guess who loses?; The taxpayers and little guys!.

Here are some words that came out of the April 3, 2008 Senate Banking Committee hearing investigating the near collapse of Bear Stearns: *"20 years ago the Fed would have let Bear Stearns go bust. Today, it is too interlinked to fail."* Not too **big** to fail..., too interlinked to fail. Which describes the world of derivatives, and hedge funds. The proliferation of a vast array of complex financial instruments that are sliced and diced and recombined in a bewildering variety of forms and bought and sold and traded by thousands of parties across the globe (and sometimes labeled 'AAA' even though backed by junk loans; can you say FRAUD) has woven everyone tightly together into one big knot. It wasn't just Bear-Stearns, but the entire system of globally interlinked financial markets and Crony Capitalism that got bailed out! Again, the Insiders win, and the People lose! 'Too **big** to fail' is a phony concept to justify bailouts. The greedy and incompetent managers get saved, as their prudent competitors pay for FIDC insurance.

The 'moral hazard' (perverse incentive) here is that Wall Street knows they will get bailed-out the next time their high-risk, highly leveraged ventures fail. Oh sure, Paulson and Bush promised 'sweeping changes' with new regulations and powers for the Fed, but the changes will be minor, and Wall Street will find a new away around them.

In Nov-2009 Sen. Dodd, Chairman of the Senate Banking Committee, unveiled a sweeping regulatory reform bill that would strip the Federal Reserve of nearly all of its power to oversee banks. It was quickly watered down.

It all comes back to the unspoken core problem; Fake Money. Without the hundreds of billions of 'liquidity' the Fed poured into the financial system since the '90s, these games couldn't be played. The toys they play with are the fake sub-prime home mortgages, plus other loose-money-based securities.

In the past, we could keep spending this fake money worldwide (by both people and government) because the USD was still the world's primary 'reserve currency' (anyone would accept it as payment, and hold assets denominated in it) because despite our problems, others have been worse (past tense; others are becoming attractive, namely the Euro, Yen, and Yuan).

The USD now has competition! Our formerly strong economy set the confidence level that the dollar won't become worthless, (but in early 2008 it started falling because the US is bankrupt due to debt and spending, with no cure in sight. For fear of starting world-wide panic by selling too much, those countries who own a lot of USD (trillions in China, Japan, etc. due to payments for exports to the US) can't afford to dump them as their value declines, but history shows us that something always triggers panic selling, and a crash in value. Due in part to its mercantilist policy of 'pegging' the yuan (at 6.83) to the falling dollar. China now leads the world in value of annual exports as of Dec-2009 (passing Germany), and also in foreign reserves at $2.4 trillion, $799 bill. (33%) of which are in US Treasury securities.

For example, as of mid 2008, individuals and businesses worldwide started to avoid transactions, investments, and savings in USD. They feared ongoing loss of market value in dollar-denominated assets. They were right, and this is how worldwide crashes in a currency can start!   As should be expected, in late-2009, China and others started to: 1. Use their own currency for international trade, and 2. Reduce their 'reserves' of USD (slowly, to avoid a panic).

Governments play the 'hold-and-hope' game with 'other people's money', but people and businesses avoid a failing currency since their own money and assets are at risk!! The crash could start from the bottom up, as merchants and producers refuse to accept US dollars !

One of the risks foreign governments fear is that the US will pay off the debt they own (U.S. bonds, etc.) by using cash created out of thin air. This would greatly reduce the value of the dollar, and is a form of default. They should be concerned. The US has huge debts (some are even 'off the books', such as future obligations of Social Security,

Medicare, etc.; see Table 1 on page 30) so our 'leaders' prefer inflation so they have more (albeit of less value) money to pay debts. Deflation (less money in circulation; more value per dollar) would help recovery from the coming depression, but that would eliminate the easy payoff of debt by the US. It's called being 'between a rock and a hard place', caused by the short-term pleasure of fake money.

Causes of the Sep-2008 Wall Street Debacle

The US economic problems have been brewing since extreme abuse of the US dollar started in 1971 with Nixon's cutting of its last link to gold. With all this fake money to play with, Congress showed its willingness to offer loans and gifts to bailout companies, industries and nations who were in trouble (and could produce votes and campaign donations) per this list (2008 $): Penn Central Railroad, 1971, $3.2; Lockheed, 1971, $1.4; Franklin Nat'l Bank, 1974, $7.8; New York City, 1975, $9.4; Chrysler, 1980, $4.0; Continental Illinois, 1984, $9.5; Savings and Loan Industry, 1989, $293.3; Mexican Gov't, 1994, $20 (the bailout money came from the ESF, see p. 45); Long-Term Capital Management L.P. (LTCM), 1998, $3.6; US Airlines, 2001, $18.6; Bear-Stearns, 2008, $30; AIG, 2008 $180; U.S. Auto Industry, 2008, $25; TARP, 2008,$700; Citigroup, 2009, $280; Bank of America, 2009, $142.2. This largesse created the 'moral hazard' of firms taking big risks on the assumption they would be bailed out if needed, and, along with lax regulation and false credit ratings, led to the crash that started in 2007.

Roberts, and Miller showed vision in their writings in A. and B. below. Stockman gives a review in C.

A. As written by **Paul Craig Roberts Ph.D.** (www.paulcraigroberts.org ; click 'articles' for archives) on May 07, 2002 in #3 'Time Running Out for the Dollar?' of his prescient seven-part series of articles 'No -Think Nation ' on America's imperiled future: *"The U.S. current account deficit is running at an annual rate of 4% of Gross Domestic Product. That's about $1 billion per day. For a number of years the large U.S. current account deficit has been accompanied by a strong dollar. Could the dollar's strength be coming to an end? Since January the dollar has declined almost 6% in value against the Euro, which has been a weak and uncertain currency since its introduction. Is this a harbinger that a large dollar overhang is beginning to worry those who are holding our currency?"*

His concerns were correct, as shown by the crash of 2008 and the plans in 2009 by other major nations to start replacing the US dollar as the primary world reserve currency. The Dec. 5, 2009 issue of the Wall Street Journal had an article 'Requiem for the Dollar' by free-market oriented Investment Advisor James Grant (grantspub.com) that confirmed the decline of the Dollar's strength, and recommended gold money as a solution to avoid further damage from government meddling.

B. Donald W. Miller, Jr., M.D. (DonaldMiller.com) warned us in his prescient article 'A Fourteen Point Plan for a Post-Wilsonian America', which he published on September 28, 2001 at www.LewRockwell.com : *"Likewise, if we do not wish to be mired in the coming economic depression for a prolonged period of time, as happened with the last one in the 1930s, which lasted twelve years, we must substantially reduce government spending, taxes, and regulatory compliance costs. Federal spending has grown eight times faster than the economy since the last depression. Over the last forty years federal expenditures on regulatory activity have increased 2.7 times faster than economy – a 14 per cent per year annual growth rate, compounded. Government regulations currently consume $977 Billion annually, siphoning off 13 per cent of the economy, which* *is $3,300.00 per man, woman, and child. In order for our country to regain economic health we must make sure that the free-market private sector once again becomes, as it was before our nation assumed the burdens of empire, the largest and fastest growing segment of the economy."*

C. David Stockman gave a lecture in March, 2011 (http://lewrockwell.com/stockman/stockman16.1.html) that revealed many details about how the 2008 crash was caused by greed and fraud since Nixon left gold in 1971. His latest book is '**The Great Deformation**', April-2013. (http://en.wikipedia.org/wiki/David_Stockman)

****

The rush of home loan defaults and bank problems started in late 2007, and peaked in Sep-2008. The underlying cause was Fed manipulation of interest rates, as described above. The excessive supply of low-interest money, delivered to lenders by the Fed and its pals at FreddieMac and FannieMae, was the 'mother's milk' of market distortion. Of course, our Wars for Empire (not defense) in Afghanistan and Iraq added to the domestic spending spree (which pours unproductive money into the economy), that we can no longer afford.

Kudos are due for leaders who raised the warning flags early, despite opposition from both Bushes and Clinton, and lack of support from 'vote-for-me' fellow Congress members. Since 1976, Rep. Ron Paul MD (R-TX-14, first elected in 1976 with 2 gaps totaling 14 years; born 1935; retired Jan-2013) was always the strongest fighter in Congress for more liberty and less government. His Libertarian philosophy calls for sound money (gold and silver in coins, paper redeemable for precious metal), and he wanted to abolish the Federal Reserve Bank (HR-2755), and associated GSEs Fannie, Freddie, the World Bank,

73

IMF, BIS, etc. He wanted to at least make the Fed subject to audit by his HR-1207, which had 317 cosponsors as of late 2009, and a similar bill S-604 in the Senate. Rep. Barney Frank did all he could to derail it, but it became an amendment on his "Financial Stability Improvement Act of 2009", bill HR-3996. Rep. Paul became Chairman of the 'Domestic and International Monetary Policy' committee in 2011, and grilled Chm. Bernanke more than once in his 2011 hearings. Former Rep. Paul introduced many bills to restore sound money, including HR 4248 on Dec. 9, 2009, the 'Free Competition in Currency Act' that would end legal tender laws and allows competing currencies. He gained mainstream support on January 19, 2010 when Pat Buchanan gave him credit for being the principled promoter of policies that are good for the US. Passage of a similar bill would be a huge step forward, and crucial to the goals of this book!

On Jan. 26, 2011, Rep. Paul introduced HR-459, the **'Federal Reserve Transparency Act of 2011',** and as of Nov. 4, 2011 it had 191 cosponsors. On the same day, a similar bill, S-202, was introduced in the Senate by his son Sen. Rand Paul (elected Nov-2010), and had 18 cosponsors. Both were described as: 'A bill to require a full audit of the Board of Governors of the Federal Reserve System and the Federal Reserve banks by the Comptroller General of the United States before the end of 2012, and for other purposes.'
On April 11, 2011, Rep. Paul introduced HR-1496 'to reform the manner in which the Board of Governors of the Federal Reserve System is audited by the Comptroller General of the United States and the manner in which such audits are reported, and for other purposes.' These three bills launched a thorough, and long overdue, audit of the Fed!

Rep. Paul retired from Congress in Jan-2013, but Rep. Paul Broun MD of GA-10 has introduced bill H.R. 24 to audit the Fed. On Feb. 4, 2013, Ron's son Sen. Rand Paul (R-Ky.) entered bill S. 209 for Fed transparency. Both men are continuing Dr. Paul's work for sound money. On Feb. 12, 2013 Sen. Paul gave the 'Tea Party' response to Pres. Obama's State of The Union' speech. Paul said all the right things about reduced spending and taxes, and the benefits of free-market capitalism. Bravo! Keep it rolling Rand!

On June 28, 2011, Sen. Jim DeMint (R-S.C.), with cosponsors Mike Lee (R-Utah) and Rand Paul (R-Ky.), introduced legislation that would exempt gold and silver coins declared by the federal or any state government as legal tender from taxation. Sen. DeMint resigned in late 2012 to become Pres. of Heritage.org, a conservative think tank, replacing Ed Feulner.

The 'Sound Money Promotion Act', S. 1287 of 2012, is meant to build on what the sponsors see as a reaction to overspending by the federal government and the falling value of the dollar. The senators said that in May, Utah became the first state to recognize these coins as legal tender within the state, and said 12 other states, including South Carolina, are considering similar measures.

As far back as 1993, legendary House Banking Committee Chairman, the late Henry B. Gonzalez (D-Texas-20, 1961-1999; lived 1916-2000), fought to make the Federal Reserve and GSEs more accountable Then in May, 2006, Sen. Chuck Hagel (R-NE, 1996-2009; born 1946), Sec. of Defense since 2013, wrote a letter, co-signed by 19 other Senators, asking Majority Leader Frisk for support of his 2005 bill S.190 'Federal Housing Enterprise Regulatory Reform Act' that would protect taxpayers from potential losses by the same GSEs. He got no support, and the bill died. Then disaster struck in 2008, as predicted!

A major facilitator to start this mess was the **Community Reinvestment Act (CRA)**, a 1977 federal law pushed by Pres. Carter that requires banks and thrifts to offer credit throughout their entire market area and prohibits them from targeting only wealthier neighborhoods with their services, a practice known as 'redlining.' The purpose of the CRA is to provide credit, including home ownership opportunities, to underserved (unqualified?) populations and commercial loans to small businesses.

The CRA was passed into law by the U.S. Congress in 1977 as a result of national grassroots pressure for affordable housing, and despite considerable opposition from the mainstream banking community. The CRA mandates that each banking institution be evaluated to determine if it has met the credit needs of its entire community. In 1995, as a result of interest from President Clinton's administration, the implementing regulations for the CRA were strengthened by focusing the financial regulators' attention on institutions' performance in helping to meet community credit needs (that is, forcing lenders to make more subprime loans!!).

The Clinton Administration's regulatory revisions with an effective starting date of January 31, 1995 were credited with substantially increasing the number and aggregate amount of loans to small businesses and to low- and moderate-income borrowers (i.e., 'subprime', unqualified!) for home loans. Part of the increase in home loans was due to increased efficiency and the genesis of lenders, like Countrywide Financial Corp. (set up as an 'off brand' by Bank of America, then purchased in Jan-2008 when CWF got in trouble), which was aggressive and did not mitigate loan risk with savings deposits (ie, borrowers must have deposits) as did traditional banks using the new subprime authorization. This is known as the secondary market for mortgage loans ('subprime', high risk for banks). The above Clinton revisions allowed the securitization of CRA loans containing subprime mortgages (ie, packaging good and bad debt (mostly mortgages) together and calling the bunch 'AAA'. These are called 'mortgage-backed securities' (MBS). This is FRAUD by the rating firms!! The first public securitization of CRA loans started in 1997 by Bear Stearns, and it helped break them in Sep-2008!. The number of CRA mortgage loans increased by 39 percent between 1993 and 1998, while other loans increased by only 17 percent (a flood of money into high risk).

As noted on P. 33, a major factor was sloppy, incomplete, fraudulent, self-serving (to get and keep customers) work by credit rating firms such as Standard and Poors, Fitch, and Moody's, who were complicit in the chain of perpetrators who falsely labeled bad debt as AAA. In 2008, the firms agreed to change their policies, but as of Feb-2013 all three firms are being investigated by the New York Attorney General over whether they breached the 2008 settlement.

In 2003, the Bush Administration recommended what the NY Times called "the most significant regulatory overhaul in the housing finance industry since the savings and loan crisis a decade ago." This change was to move governmental supervision of two of the primary agents guaranteeing subprime loans, Fannie Mae and Freddie Mac under a new agency created within the Department of the Treasury. However, it did not alter the implicit guarantee that Washington will bail the companies out if they run into financial difficulty. That perception enabled them to issue debt at significantly lower rates than their competitors. The changes were generally opposed along Party lines and eventually failed to happen

Among banks and the regulatory agencies, there was a consensus that data collection, recordkeeping, and reporting requirements imposed a heavy burden on small community institutions. As a result of a 2002 review of the CRA regulations, and revision of an initial Federal Deposit Insurance Corporation (FDIC) proposal following a public commenting period that was largely negative, the FDIC, Office of the Comptroller of the Currency (OCC) and the Federal Reserve Board (FRB), made substantive changes to the implementation of regulations for the CRA for banks (not Thrifts). Credit for portions of above two paragraphs to: (http://en.wikipedia.org/wiki/Community_Reinvestment_Act) .

In the 1980s, groups such as the activists at ACORN ('Association of Community Organizations for Reform Now', www.acorn.org) began pushing charges of "redlining" - claims that banks discriminated against minorities in mortgage lending. In 1989, sympathetic members of Congress got the **Home Mortgage Disclosure Act** amended to force banks to collect racial data on mortgage applicants. This allowed various studies to be ginned up that seemed to validate the original accusation.

In fact, minority mortgage applications were rejected more frequently than other applications - but the overwhelming reason wasn't racial discrimination, but simply that minorities tend to have weaker finances. A study in 1992 proved that bias was not the problem. Yet the harm was done and banks loosened their rules to avoid lawsuits.

The **'Troubled Assets Relief Program' (TARP)** was a 3-page note introduced by Paulson and Bush in Oct-2008 in a panic mode based on predictions of a sudden crash in the economy. They wanted $500 billion with no questions asked, and no liability. Congress converted it to a pork-laden 500+ page tome that still had little oversight. They and the recipients have refused to account for how the first

$385 bill. was spent! The so-called 'panic' urgency is now being viewed by many as a lie used by Paulson and Bush to bail out firms run by their friends and campaign donors, and the voters who own their stock. It is grossly unfair to well-managed firms who now must continue to fight rescued competitors (run by greedy jerks or fools) who should have failed. Similar problems and bailouts occurred in Europe. Only Iceland; a. let their banks fail, so the losses fell on managers and investors rather than citizens, and b. prosecuted managers for fraud. The economy is recovering well.

A new book, 'Financing Failure: A Century of Bailouts', by Vern McKinley, was issued on Jan. 10, 2012. His research shows how the financial crisis starting in 2008 was caused by the government and Fed due to their years of meddling with the money supply, interest rates, and subsidies, then made worse by bailouts for political 'friends'.

The huge debts incurred by the Treasury and Fed to pay for the bailouts have created a large risk of future reduction in value of the US dollar due monetary inflation. Stay tuned!

The Bad News

Here is the bad news about possible collapse of the US Economy and Dollar, and how to protect yourself.

1. Walter J. "John" Williams has been a private consulting economist and a specialist in government economic reporting for more than 25 years. He started 'Shadow Government Statistics' (http://www.shadowstats.com/) in 2004 because government reporting was so false and incomplete. In an Aug-2010 interview article 'Economy Heading for a Systemic Collapse into Hyperinflationary Great Depression' (http://www.marketoracle.co.uk/Article21676.html) he

discusses how the failing US economy and Dollar could soon descend into sudden hyperinflation (loss of over 90% of purchasing power of dollar in a few days), and force people to barter for food and supplies. Unlike the 2007 start of hyperinflation in Zimbabwe, where they used dollars as a 'backup' currency, the US has no such choice. He predicts barter and chaos, with precious metal becoming the only useful 'money', valued by weight, until the government gets settled (in some form; fascist, ultra-liberal, etc.??). He recommends having a month or two of food (canned, dried) and a means to purify water for survival until things (food stores, banks) start working again.

2. Similar predictions have been made by Dr. Marc Faber, of Marc Faber Ltd. (http://www.gloomboomdoom.com/).

3. Dr. Paul Craig Roberts (www.paulcraigroberts.org) sees the possibility of neighborhood self-defense clans emerging from the chaos in 'The Year America Dissolved' (http://www.vdare.com/roberts/100726_dissolved.htm). In his articles 'The Collapsing US Economy ' (http://www.informationclearinghouse.info/article21714.htm, 'The End of American Hegemony (http://www.creators.com/opinion/paul-craig-roberts/the-end-of-american-hegemony.html), and 'How the US Economy Was Lost' http://informationclearinghouse.info/article22087.htm), he finds a major depression likely.

4. In 2002, Congress created the military 'US Northern Command' (NorthCom) to 'work with' local police nationwide for homeland defense. Guess who ends-up in charge ? (Clue: The Army with its bigger staff, equipment, and political power) See http://www.northcom.mil/about/index.html). This is an unprecedented incursion of the military into domestic law enforcement! They expect 'social unrest' as more people

worry about the War on Terror, and now (2013) about lost jobs, homes, and maybe soon, hunger. Arrests will be made simply for complaining loudly. Major detention camps (jails) have been built to hold 'troublemakers'. Martial law will be imposed whenever the Feds want it; they have the laws all set-up! Michael Edwards says it well in 'The Ultimate Betrayal: Police and Military Working Together to Oppress Americans'; see http://www.activistpost.com/2010/08/ultimate-betrayal-police-and-military.html . "The concepts of military service and public police service are worlds apart, for good reason. Today in America, we are currently witnessing the culmination of a decades-long trend that has introduced the language, weapons, and tactics of the overseas battlefield onto the streets of America."

5. In Feb-2012, Wyoming legislators proposed a plan to study what the state should do in the event of a complete economic and/or political collapse in the United States. It would create a state-run government 'continuity task force', which would prepare Wyoming for potential catastrophes, from disruptions in food and energy supplies, loss of police and fire services, etc., and the need to issue its own alternative currency. In Jan-2013 state Rep. Kendell Kroeker wrote a bill nullifying Obama's gun control laws, and making it a crime, subject to arrest, for the Feds to come into WY to enforce it, saying; "We've got a right to make our laws, and if the federal government is going to try to enforce unconstitutional laws on our people and take away the rights of Wyoming citizens, then we as a state are going to step up and make that a crime."

6. I suggest that survival gear, including storable food and water (with purification supplies), a wood-burning stove, matches, medical kit, guns for self-defense and hunting, and pre-1964 US 'junk' silver coins (usable for bullion value

when paper money crashes), and a crank-powered radio (with cell phone charger cable) will be needed.

****

The above bad news fits the pattern of a declining empire, and thus applies to Empire-USA. To see my essays on this, and other topics, go to my archive at ActivistPost.com, scroll to bottom of Home page and select 'Contributors', then my name.

As discussed on page 29 (see 'Key Point'), the crash of the US economy and dollar have been delayed by the fact that the dollar is the world's primary reserve currency (held by others as 'good as gold'), and countries that own a lot of dollars (China, Japan, S. Korea, etc.) don't want it to crash. However they are also tired of our abuse where we create dollars out of thin air to pay for imports and debts. Conversely, other nations must buy dollars to pay for most imports, and face declining exchange rates if they have expanded their money supply too much.
As the bond and securities markets decline in value and dividends, we will see serious problems in funding of life insurance and pensions that had 'overly optimistic' funding plans based on returns of 8 to 10 percent.

It all comes back to how distortions of the free-market by the government always do more harm than good, often to the intended beneficiaries. Very few people understand, or care about, the above economic and currency issues. They prefer bread and circuses, as we crash!! SAD.

Politicians Use Fake Money to Keep Their Jobs

Politicians hate to have the government run out of money. They need it to fund projects as gifts to voters and

82

campaign donors that help them win elections, and continue their lush lifestyles of fun and power. Most are ushers at the trough; 'Slip me $5 and come to the front of the line and get $100 from the trough.' A good return on investment ! This is why political campaigns raise and spend so much money; the donors give it (a bribe) in expectation of a big payback ! This is true of any country, but is worst when there is a central bank to provide fake money for paybacks (fake base-metal coins and paper have no redeemability to a commodity such as gold).

As discussed on p.21, our central bank, the unconstitutional, privately owned, secretive, banking industry cartel called the 'Federal Reserve System' (Fed), was created secretly by bankers for long-term control of the financial system and profits, and also to fund wars (the '1812', 1845 'Mexican-American', 1861 'Civil', and 1898 'Spanish-American' wars all had funding problems). The 'war goods' industry (Ike's 'military-industrial complex') views wars as good business, despite the death and destruction. This evil motive is justified by slogans like 'stop killer dictators', 'spread democracy', 'preemptive defense', and other fake excuses. Some say they pressured 'pacifist' Wilson to enter WW1 to assure their customers England and France won and could pay their debts to them. In fact they help start wars; was the sinking of the Lusitania by a German U-Boat a planned trigger? Did someone leak to the Germans that it was carrying munitions to England?

Having easy access to money makes it easier for governments to start or enter wars, instead of negotiating a settlement or minding their own business! As shown in Appendix 2 on page 129, all of our wars since the 1776 Revolution have been started by lies from DC to serve economic and political goals, not homeland defense. This is an abuse of our troops and economy, but is good for the power lust and re-election of politicians!

Governments almost ALWAYS abuse access to an unlimited supply of money by creating too much, thereby reducing, or destroying, its purchasing power. Since the Fed started in 1913, the US dollar's (USD) purchasing power has dropped by over 95% (20:1)!

Since Fed Chm. Bernanke started pumping money into the U.S. government (and the world) in 2008, he has been buying U.S. Treasury bonds (which creates new money) at fake low interest rates. As Peter Schiff said in his March 1, 2013 'Gold Letter' (europacmetals.com); *" The Fed is expected to buy nearly 90% of new Treasury bonds in 2013, according to Bloomberg. This is a tremendous subsidy that has kept 10-year Treasury yields below 1.95% on average this year so far. Last year, with 10-year yields averaging 1.8%, the Treasury spent $360 billion on interest payments alone. That was nearly 10% of all expenditures. Let's assume a Fed tightening causes these rates to triple - not unreasonable for a government facing over 100% debt-to-GDP. If these rates triple by 2015, and another $2 trillion or so is added to the debt, then interest would make up over 30% of annual federal expenditures; Just interest. Then, there are principal repayments, Medicare/Medicaid, Social Security, the Armed Forces, and all the other entitlements for which the Treasury is responsible. Is DC going to default on our creditors, our seniors, or our men and women in uniform? "* (see Table 1, p.30).

The self-serving, lying, politicians and economists (99% are) modify measures like GDP and unemployment to make things look better. They claimed 'green shoots' were showing back in March-2009! Paul Craig Roberts Ph.D. wrote 'The Missing Recovery' on March 1, 2013 (click 'Articles' at; PaulCraigRoberts.org) to point out the truth.

All this money creation is done to cover spending by Congress, but is destroying the value, and Reserve

Currency status, of the USD, so is unsustainable and leading to devastating higher rates and costs! As I write in March-2013, the Dems and Repubs are screaming like children to blame each other for our fiscal mess. 'Cliff' talk has been replaced by 'sequestration'. Another form of fake money (the IMF 'CDR'?) is being discussed to replace the failing USD, but gold is also being viewed as money by more banks, governments and people. The next few years will be very interesting!

Those few people who warn of such abuse, and tout the gold standard as the solution, are called kooks and dinosaurs by the elite in power, who also call gold a 'barbarous relic'. This elite includes most 'economists' since they are dependent on government funds for their jobs.

A classic 'elite' family is the Rockefellers. They spent millions (from Standard Oil) on philanthropy, but also sought power in world politics and banking. To promote central banking (and its benefits to them), the Rockefeller's started a plan in 1902 called 'The General Education Board' to pay 'grants' to professors who would support the concept of central banking and our Fed. Note on page 22 that Sen. Nelson Aldrich, who headed the commission that designed the Fed structure, was father-in-law of J. D. Rockefeller Jr. Rockefeller's academic empire included the University of Chicago, which he cofounded in 1890, that is known as home of the 'Monetarist School' which endorses management of monetary system by central banks (see Glossary page 135). David Rockefeller was Chairman of Chase-Manhattan bank until 1981, and remains a leader there and in the Council on Foreign Relations and the Trilateral Commission (see p.53) to manipulate money and politics. Henry Kissinger and Zbigniew Brzezinski were two of his 'operatives'.

Since the 1930's (when Keynes arrived) the academic economics profession has been united on only one topic: the superiority of central banking to the gold standard. That's how they get published, tenure, and grants. The politicians like the associated 'stimulus' spending as a way to do favors to get votes and campaign donations. Follow the money and hubris! Support of central banking is basic to the entire university curriculum in modern economics worldwide.

Critics of the gold standard point out that gold's price varies widely. In his Dec. 3, 2011 report, Gary North (garynorth.com) says: ' *Excuse me? The gold market today establishes the price of gold in terms of fiat money systems run by central banks. So, the price of gold as denominated in fiat money varies mainly because the value of currencies fluctuates wildly.* ' **This is a KEY POINT because this book recommends pricing in 'weight of gold', which produces stable pricing, and there is no 'price of gold', just an 'exchange rate' with other money.**

Lewis Lehrman said it well starting on page 12 of the first edition (Aug-2011) of his book 'The True Gold Standard'; '*The test of what will endure as honest money can only be studied in the empirical laboratory of human history; mathematical abstractions, drawn from the blackboards of academic economists, will not do.*' The trouble with 'academics' is that they live in an unaccountable world as to results of their meddling with fiat money (inflation, bubbles, wars, corruption, etc.). Bernanke's money-flooding will soon be seen as a failure, and he will retire and say 'I tried'!

It has been a fun party since the Bretton Woods Agreement in 1944 made the USD the official 'worlds' reserve currency', and then our de facto status since 1971, allowed us to print money to pay our bills, and borrow to excess. Watch out, our era of financing wars, Empire-USA, foreign aid, imports, and homeland spending with fake money is about to end!

Chapter 4: Use of Gold as Money

Why Gold?

All forms of money serve as a 'medium of exchange', and 'unit of account', which is convenient and flexible compared to barter. **Key Point:** Note that when a valuable commodity (such as gold) is used as money ('monetization of gold'), the money is worth as much as the goods or services in the transaction. This is also true of barter, but with gold's high value per weight and volume, etc. (see the nine characteristics on P. 92), using gold is more convenient, and thus helps improve commerce. Two more benefits of using commodity money are to; 1. Limit excessive expansion of the money supply (inflation; loss of value) by the government, and 2. Provide a market-based, and stable, store and measure of value. This system needs no government controls except inspections (which could be by a private org) to verify mints indeed have the gold reserves they claim to for redeemability. The commodity could be (and has been) wheat, iron, diamonds, notched sticks, or pearls, but the market (users of money) usually chooses gold because it works best for the reasons shown in 'Redick's First Monetary Rule' on page 92. Thus, it will be used as the 'presumed market choice' in this book. Silver and copper supplies and costs are more volatile than gold (more new production, are consumed for industrial use, etc.), so are less attractive, but useable.

As also discussed on page 92, paper 'money certificates' and token coins (base metal) can be used as a convenience (cheap to make, light weight, avoid loss of gold due to wear, etc.) but users of this 'representative money' will insist the money must be marked on its face as to how much gold it represents (weight and fineness) and be redeemable for that amount on demand by any bearer at the issuing bank or mint. Further, users will insist the bank or mint must disclose to the public (via lobby poster, mail to depositors, Internet web site, etc.) that it has enough gold in its' reserves (physically; with no encumbering liens or leases) to redeem 100% of the 'representative money' (paper notes) it has in circulation. Without these conditions, and in the absence of legal tender laws, people (the 'market') will not use such representative money, and will seek better money from another mint. Competition will produce good money!

When gold is used as money, it has no 'price' in dollars, yen, etc. Weight is the **unit of account** (such as milligrams). Sellers will set prices in weight of gold. **There will be prices IN weight of gold, but not OF gold! (Example again; What is the price of a dollar?). Gold money will have an 'exchange rate' with other money, but not a 'price'. This will take some getting used to as we evolve to pricing in weight of gold.**

History shows us that when countries use sound money (such as gold coins, or paper and tokens as redeemable receipts for gold) they have zero or low inflation, zero or minor 'cycles' of economic panic or depression, and more peace, liberty, and prosperity (smaller governments). For example, the number of grams of gold needed to buy a barrel of oil has been very steady over the years. Thus, we would expect all countries to use sound money, except the leaders want more money than they can get by just taxing, especially for wars. They want a way to create money 'out of thin air'. Fiat paper money (not redeemable for gold; we call ours 'Federal Reserve Notes') serves this purpose. Even when some level of redeemability exists, governments often 'suspend' it before, during, and after wars (the US did for the Revolutionary, 1812, and Civil wars), and then must be pushed to restore it (often with less value).

The US ended the right for other nations (FDR took it from mere people in 1933) to redeem paper dollars for gold when Nixon abrogated the Bretton Woods Agreement on August 15, 1971 due to our serious financial problems such as; a. We were running out of gold; France and others were redeeming their 'Euro-Dollars' to gold (USDs accumulated in Europe due to our postwar spending and loans there); b. The US was poor after spending on Vietnam and LBJ's 'Great Society'. Under this pressure, Nixon illegally 'floated' the USD (no fixed-price for gold; no fixed exchange rates with foreign currency), and ended redeemability of Fed Notes to gold by any person or government. This meant the US could make dollars out of thin air at will, and did we ever! Due to this increase in the money supply, the dollar's value has fallen by 82% since 1971 (5 to 1; per CPI by Bureaus of Labor Statistics), and over 98% since the Fed started in 1913 (50 to 1); Thus prices are higher, because the dollar is 'worth less' (two words).. This is a ripoff of most people because their incomes do not increase as fast as price inflation, and their savings are worth less. As a result, more wives are working, spending and debt replace saving, and speculative, leveraged, buying of homes and securities increases.

Again, the main purpose using gold as money ('notes' and base-metal tokens are not money, but just claim checks, or receipts, for gold held by the mint who issued them) is to prevent excessive expansion of the money supply ('monetary inflation') by the government or private mints, and thus reduction in purchasing power. Without redeemability for gold, this 'fiat money' is an unlimited 'piggy-bank' and credit card for the government or mints. History and logic shows **the government cannot be trusted to not abuse money creation.** The excessive money has allowed damaging, unconstitutional, corrupting, massive increases in government spending for wars, welfare, and pork. It has also created the growth in the number of lobbyists seeking favors. Prices started to rise a few years after 1971 as the effect of excessive money and spending trickled to the US economy, and most increased by a factor of 5 to 8 by 2011. By 1975, all nations worldwide ceased redeemability, even the prudent Swiss floated the Swiss franc (SF) in 2000, but have been less abusive than others. Hence while 1 USD = about 4 SF in 1961, it is now about 1 US = 1 SF, so they only inflated by 2.5 while by 2008 the US inflated by 10; four times more!

The US has been the worst abuser among developed nations (older countries remembered their lessons from past monetary failures). Again, the US has created so much new 'free, fake money' since 1971 that the USD has lost 80% of its purchasing power since then (this excessive expansion of the money supply is called 'monetary inflation', like a balloon) with its consequent price increases (due to loss of the Dollars' purchasing power) called 'price inflation'. Check prices of common 'commodity' items (that are not imported, subsidized, cheaper due to new technology, or under price control), such as a pizza, a restaurant meal, or even a car. Good examples are: 1. A room at a 'Motel 6' cost $6 in the 1950s but is now in the $50 range in 2013 (same type of room and service), and 2. A family car cost about $2,000 in the '60s but is now about $20,000 in 2013. There is your 8 to 10X loss of USD value since the late 1940's (when the post-war big-spending started)! This goes along with a 98% loss since the Federal Reserve monopoly was created in 1913!

The only reason we can get away with this is because the USD is the world's primary 'reserve currency' (held by banks as 'good as gold' reserves; any person, firm, or bank will take and keep it as if 'good as gold'; example- when nations buy and sell from each other, they use mostly USD, but this is changing! - see P. 59), because it is viewed as a share in 'USA, Inc.', the world's strongest economy, which sadly is fading (faster since 2007) as we continue the long abuse of our economy (by spending, taxing, and harmful intervention 'management' by the Fed and government) and money (by excessive expansion of the supply). The era of US world dominance is ending, as it does with all empires.

History shows us that the use of 'real money' (made of a commodity with market value such as gold, with its 'representative' paper 'notes' or base-metal tokens redeemable for gold by bearer, on demand) is fundamental to the long-term success and survival of a nation. 'Fake Money', paper and base-metal coins created and 'managed' by a central bank (ours is the Federal Reserve System; 'the Fed') is what allows the massive spending and debt for wars and domestic pork and welfare. The pork and grants have corrupted the ethics of our federal government ('Here's some pork, vote for me.'), and the states, citizens, business, universities, and academics, etc. who happily accept it. Congresspersons brag on their web sites about how much pork they have obtained for their districts or states. This 2-way corruption is a fatal sign of a failing Empire.

Redick's Four Monetary Rules

I offer below, **'Redick's Four Monetary Rules'** to describe the requirements for a monetary system using 'real money' (money made of a valuable commodity). The market has historically chosen the commodity based on the 10 characteristics shown below (in Rule 1) which are best satisfied by a valuable metallic commodity such as gold, silver, or copper. Hence, this book uses them for discussion and examples. However, private mints could offer any commodity as money, and let the market (money users) decide what they prefer.

First Rule: Money can be in any form, but this analysis will discuss coins and paper notes

A. Coins, which can be of two types;
1. 'Commodity', where they are partly or wholly made of a commodity such as gold or silver. Various coin values would have different amounts. For example, a small, round, gold disc could be forged into a hole in the center of a coin. This would allow testing to assure its purity and weight. The balance of the coin would be hard base metal or alloy, with the weight of precious metal the coin contains marked on it, or
2. 'Representative' (or 'Token'), where they are made of base metals such as copper, aluminum, zinc, nickel, steel, and alloys thereof, and are marked as redeemable to a certain weight and purity of a commodity such as gold or silver. These are useful for lower value transactions.
****

Table 2
To achieve broad use, commodity coins must be made of, or contain, a material that has these ten characteristics:

1) Rare, with a low amount in existence now, and limited new supply,
2) Malleable; can be pressed/stamped into coins,
3) Stable physically and chemically; doesn't break, rust, or rot; can be stored; lasts through much handling,
4) Easy to identify, and determine purity and weight,
5) Difficult or impossible to counterfeit,
6) Homogeneous; a piece is the same throughout,
7) Divisible into pieces; diamonds and pearls aren't,
8) High value per ounce; not bulky to handle or store, and
9) Acceptable to most Sellers; familiar and saleable.
10) Has market value when not used as money. Thus is; a) equal in value to the good or service in a transaction, and
   b) a store and measure of value (Purchasing Power).

The 'market' (users of money) has decided that gold fits these requirements best, but silver and copper can have a role in parallel, with no fixed ratios set as to value per gram (i.e., no bi-metallic standard). The coins must be valued and marked by weight of their precious metal content (such as 'milligrams'), or the amount they can be redeemed for. It is interesting to note that gold is not 'consumed' as other commodities, including silver and copper, are. Thus except for wear, over 90% of all gold mined in history still exists (even if buried in a tomb).

Approximately 160,000 metric tonnes of gold have been mined in all history. The aggregate un-mined known reserves of all the world's gold mining companies is approximately 45,000 tonnes. Gold is being mined at about 2,600 tonnes a year, so the above-ground supply is expanding at 1.6% per annum.

A 'best estimate' of gold ownership by major nations and consortiums (all need audit) through Oct-2012 is shown in Tables 2 and 3 on pages 108 and 109, plus the IMF 2,814 tonnes, ECB 502 tonnes, and 102 other nations for a total of 30,563 tonnes (data from www.marketoracleco.uk, and Spiegel.de). For more info, go to www.resourceinvestor.com. If the IMF is dissolved, one would assume its gold would be distributed to its 186 shareholders, of which the US is by far the largest with 16.79 percent of the ownership and votes (Japan is #2 at only 6.02 %). On this basis, the US could own another 478.3 tonnes.

There is always 'enough' gold for money, because if a nation's economy (GDP) grows faster than its gold supply, the increased demand will cause their gold for domestic transactions to **APPRECIATE** in purchasing power. The same logic applies to the world economy. It is self-adjusting and needs no government meddling!

B. Paper: A **'representative' note** is just a 'receipt' or 'claim check' for precious metal, and must be; 1) Valued and marked by the weight or amount of the commodity it represents. No 'name', such as 'dollar', is needed, and 2) Redeemable for such commodity by the Bearer upon a demand to the Issuer (mint or bank) of the paper at Issuer's various premises, with such locations publicized (via Internet web site, sales literature, etc.).

Second Rule: No government laws shall apply to control the Issuers, foreign or domestic, of coins and paper notes, except to assure full disclosure of percent content of precious and base metal (hard metals may be included to decrease wear) of issued coins, and ready access for inspection of the amount, purity, and legal status (owned, not leased, or encumbered) of physical precious metal in their possession to redeem notes and tokens.

Third Rule: Money issued by the government, if any, shall have no special status, or privilege, over money issued by persons, or privately owned firms. Such money would be issued by the nation's Treasury Department, and there would be no 'central bank'.

Fourth Rule: There will be no designated 'world reserve currency', set by agreement between nations, but such status might exist de facto due to free market usage. Thus, buyers and sellers will decide which are the 'preferred' currencies, and fake or debased money will be avoided. Examples of former primary world reserve currencies are the French franc, British pound, and now the US dollar (which is approaching 'former' or 'reduced' status).

****

In the US, the above rules would require abolition of the legal tender laws (as a start), and a law that mints (or banks acting as mints) must hold 100% gold reserves to redeem all paper notes, or base metal tokens, in circulation. As to gold reserves for banks, I recommend that 'demand deposits' (checking) be required to have 100% reserves, and 'time deposits' have reserve ratios (40 to 60%?) based on prudence of the bank managers and approval of their customers (or they will withdraw their funds or sell the stock). Banks would be free of government control (including foreign bank branches in the U.S., starting a new bank, and multi-state banking), but would be required to publicly disclose their reserves, loan amounts, and other obligations that affect solvency. State-owned banks offer an interesting step away from the Fed. North Dakota (banknd.nd.gov) has had a successful one since 1919, and others states are considering having one (and using gold and silver coins; check Utah).

The goal is to engage in a transition to real money in the US, then promote the same transition worldwide. This is likely to work, because fake money, or money from issuers with inadequate reserves of gold for redeemability, will, 1. soon be refused as payment, 2. be discounted (the Seller will ask a higher price to accept it), or 3. not be held as savings or investments. This shows the error in Gresham's Law which states 'bad money drives out good'. It does not consider 1, 2 and 3 above, because it only applies where the exchange rate between currencies is fixed by law, and legal tender laws exist.

Results from the Rules

Some of the results of using these Rules are;

A. Stable Purchasing Power: Purchasing Power will be stable, or increase, in the long-term (hundreds of years), with; 1) possible minor and gradual decreases as new gold is mined, or 2) increases (appreciation) if some of the existing supply is taken out of circulation, or as economic activity grows, causing an increase in demand for the existing supply of gold. The appreciation is a positive incentive to save, and avoid debt. For example, gold is now (Mar. 1, 2013) worth near $1,580 per oz., so it would take about 12 oz. to buy a modest car (with current 'dollar' pricing). Maybe after 20 years on the gold standard, it will take only 6 oz. to buy a car (we hope things are priced in 'weight of gold' by then, not 'dollars'). This subject is discussed in depth in Nobel Laureate F. A. Hayek's 'Denationalization of Money: The Argument Refined', 1976, which puts forth the case to; 1) end the government monopoly on money creation, 2) let anyone create money, and 3) let the free market determine which type of money is used (just as I suggest in 'Monetary Rules' above). The point is to end government politicalization, abuse, and fraud in creation of money. Remember, the plan is to get rid of currency 'names', and just label them as to the weight of gold. The sooner we change, the better.

B. Reduction of Excessive Spending, and Its Damage: With real money, people, firms and governments will not be able to engage in excessive spending very long because they will run out of money. This gives incentive for them to engage in honest, rational, positive acts such as; spend carefully, save, and plan ahead. As a result there will be; 1) fewer and smaller wars; 2) no major bubbles in housing, Silicon Valley, or Wall Street; 3) less welfare, pork, subsidies, etc. which make people, schools and firms dependent on DC money, and attract lobbyist to 'buy' legislators so they can get favors. A nice side-effect is that most lobbyists will go out of business because their will be little or no pork and subsidies available from DC; also, when the 'paybacks' get low, campaign funding will be less, so campaigns will be cheaper, and more 'normal' people will be able to run for office; and 4) no excessive imports, and resultant 'off-shoring' of US jobs, factories, and professionals, because there will be no unlimited supply of fake money, injected into the economy by the Fed, to fund these payments to foreign suppliers! Again, this can only be carried to extremes by the issuer of the world's primary reserve currency; for now the USA. These limits will be automatic. Some will say, this is a loss of needed 'liquidity' and 'flexibility', but I say it is a good brake on unfettered (dare I use the Liberal's pejorative?) spending.

****

The result is a positive incentive to save, and avoid debt, due to **APPRECIATION of purchasing power** of the money, a concept that people today have never seen because all nations use fiat money. Econ 101 tells us that a commodity (such as gold) in limited supply, and with increasing demand for it (growth of the economy), will APPRECIATE in value. **This has huge importance because it kills the 'there is not enough gold' argument!!** Appreciation of value is; a. ignored by most economists and b. suppressed, or unknown to, all politicians (they love paying debts and avoiding taxation by expanding the money supply with fake money -- monetary inflation – and paying debts with low value money).

Notice that part 'B-4)' above solves the problem of excessive imports causing loss of jobs due to off-shoring of factories. With the finite supply of real money, US importers will find themselves, and their banks, getting short of money, and import less. Demand will increase for domestic producers, and the money will stay in the same country. Free trade is good, unless importing is taken to extremes by the use of fake money. Note again, this can only happen if the fake money is also the world's reserve currency (until demoted!). Poor citizens in third-world countries which have little 'real money' to buy imports, will have incentive to work hard, innovate, and earn gold from exports.

Many articles have been written about causes and cures of the current economic crash since it started in late 2007. Politicians want various versions of 'stimulus' (more spending) to fix a problem caused by too much money in the economy. This will make things worse after a few months of fun spending. What they should do is cut taxes, end wars and empire, end all subsidies, end the Dept. of Education, Homeland Security, Commerce, Agriculture, and others, and take broad measures to reduce government spending. Free-market capitalism will rise from the ashes, and produce honest, sustainable, jobs, peace, and prosperity. Pres. Obama, N. Klein, R. Reich, P. Krugman, and others whine that 'capitalism was tried and failed'. What a joke! The US economy has had a declining percent of capitalism since fake money was started in 1913, and the above positive benefits of capitalism have fallen even faster since the end of partial-gold backing of our money in 1971. It is Socialism that has harmed us most since 1913.

I don't underestimate the difficulty of, and opposition to, a transition to gold as money. Some will say we should set less ambitious goals, but I say these lesser goals are just steps along the way and we must never stop striving for the ultimate goal of eradicating the government from our monetary system.

Maybe if we hit bottom hard enough (2015, 2020?) in the current depression people and the government will start to listen to us 'real money' folks, and go for the gold.

Former U. S. Rep. Ron Paul was a leader for many years in the fight for 'sound money' and compliance with the Constitution as to reduced spending and intervention at home and abroad. Former U.S. Sen. Chuck Hagel issued warnings in 2004 and 2005 about impending trouble at the GSEs, but was ignored. Bravo to these leaders, plus P. C.

Roberts Ph. D., and others shown on the list of authors quoted in this book, starting on page 121.

Because the Fed gives it an unlimited supply of funding, the U.S. Federal government has become an arrogant master that dominates and abuses its citizens, the U.S. States, and other countries (by jerking the purse strings), while providing big incomes and privileges to those people and firms that have ready access to it. Our national disease is that it is deemed 'normal' to have the government supply whatever is 'nice', 'good', 'needed', or 'wanted', and most people want/expect 'somebody else' to pay for it ('the rich'). This parasitic mode of living is immoral and unsustainable, and reveals the classic signs of decadence in a failing empire.

Fighting the system is hard, but I predict Ghandhi's aphorism will prevail: **"First they ignore you, then they ridicule you, then they fight you, then you win."**

Two Plans to Convert the USA to Gold As Money

#1: The Five-Step 'Top-Down' plan is an approach where Congress votes to make the changes. (see text below)
#2: The 'Bottom-Up' plan is led by the States (see p. 107)
Plan 2 has a better chance of being implemented.

Description of Plan #1: It was first published in Jan-2010, and has my original ideas, but builds on the work and concepts from Founder Charles H. Carroll (1794–1865, U.S. Congressman for New York); Ludwig von Mises (1881-1973; mises.org); F. A. Hayek (1899-1992); Prof. J. Salerno (1950-) in his Sep-1982 Policy Analysis No. 16 'The Gold Standard: An Analysis of Some Recent

Proposals' for Cato Institute (www.Cato.org); Murray Rothbard (1926-1995) in his 1991 book 'The Case for a 100% Gold Dollar'; former U.S. Rep. Ron Paul M.D (1935-) and his many House Resolutions, speeches, books, and essays; Lewis Lehrman's work since he co-chaired Reagan's 'Gold Commission' with Dr. Paul in 1981, his Aug-2011 book 'The True Gold Standard', and his site www.TheGoldStandardNow.org; and Dr. Edwin Vieira, Jr.,'Pieces of Eight'. Author Doug Casey has been a strong promoter of gold as money (caseyresearch.com; see page 121). There are many more supporters of gold-as-money, so please forgive the omissions. Mises noted the true advantage of a gold standard when he said; 'a managed fiat money must become a plaything of politics.' My plan ends the government and Fed monopoly on control and issuance of money, and makes 'weight of gold' the unit of account. Read on for more details on how to implement the transition to gold, and the benefits to expect.

There have been three 'mainstream' (recognized by academics and the government) types of gold standards in the past; **1. Gold Specie, 2. Gold Exchange**, and **3. Gold Bullion**. See the Glossary on page 140 for details.

I now re-introduce number **4.** the **'Private Gold Standard'.** I say 're-introduce' because the 'mainstream' academics and the government folks have ignored or ridiculed past essays on the topic. Maybe this is because the bureaucrats' jobs and social life depend on being 'mainstream'. Pathetic! Several versions are discussed in Salerno's 1982 'Cato Analysis 16' shown above, and a similar approach in the Paul-Lehrman report, 'Case for Gold', 1982. My version is based on **'Redick's Four Monetary Rules'** shown on page 91, and implemented by the **Five-Step Plan** shown below. While other private gold standards include 'parallel government currency' and other remnants of the monopoly and Fed system, **my version**

has zero mandatory (but some optional) control by the government, and banks. The Fed will be gone! Notice that under this plan money is produced by private firms in the free market where customers (users of money) decide which source and type of money is best, and mints compete for customers by supplying a good product. There is no Fed, and government mints (run by the Treasury), if any, are optional, and have no control or privilege over the private mints. The free market is allowed to work!

The Five-Step 'Top Down' Plan:

Step 1. Repeal: a. All legal tender laws so private firms (mints) can issue new money, b. Laws that tax increase in market value (then to be known as 'purchasing power') of precious-metal coins (formerly considered numismatic), and c. Any other laws that prevent, inhibit, or tax the new money. The only government role would be to prevent fraud (including counterfeiting), and to verify by physical inspection that reserves are as advertised (but with no reserve 'requirements'). Again, I recommend that 'demand deposits' (checking) have 100% reserves, and 'time deposits' have reserve ratios based on prudence of bankers and approval of their customers (or they will withdraw their funds or sell the stock). The Federal Reserve will be abolished three to five years after private money becomes legal (or if Congress refuses abolishment, let it atrophy to death from lack of customers and income). Its useful functions could be done by private firms.

Step 2. Private mints are allowed, with government licensing optional. Banks could also provide mint services. As discussed on pages 87 and 91, silver, semi-precious metals, and foreign coins could be used (based on market demand), but for simplicity, only use of gold will be discussed here. The mints would introduce new gold money labeled by law as to the weight and purity (fineness) of gold a coin contains, or that redeemable tokens or paper certificates represent (thus 'weight' is the unit of account). Some might offer 'Digital Gold Currency' (see goldmoney.com). All mints would be required by law to; 1. Publicize the weight and purity of gold they have as a reserve for redeeming paper or digital money, and the value of money issued, 2. Allow unscheduled physical inspections to confirm that the gold is in their possession, and free of encumbrances such as liens, leases, etc. The same would apply to base-metal coins. The 'unscheduled' requirement will prevent relocating the same gold to be put on display at different mints, or their branches, 'just in time' for an inspection! The results of these inspections would be published by the mint's Internet web site, newspaper, poster in the mint, etc., and available from a government web site. The inspections would be justified as a routine function of the government to prevent fraud, but could be done by a private org. Mints with strong reserves will advertise their strength to attract customers. Customers will 'wake up' and pay attention to reserve status, rather than assuming the government is protecting them with regulations. **The free market at work!**

Step 3. Require the Federal Reserve banks, the U.S. Treasury (Ft. Knox), the Exchange Stabilization Fund, and any other part of the United States government that has gold, to promptly submit to a private audit of the amount and purity of gold they own and its title status (leased?, loaned?), reveal the results to the public, and then give it all to a 'Redemption Trust' owned by the U.S. Treasury, to be used to redeem existing coin or paper currency, 'digital deposits', and bonds (such as M3, see page 42) on demand, based on a certain weight per Dollar, in accordance with the plan below. The Fed would not be involved in such conversions. Some may argue that the Fed is a private firm and owns the gold it has, but this ignores the fact that it got it from the US citizens illegally in the first place by issuing fake Fed Notes, and perhaps some from FDR's confiscation of gold in 1933 (see ESF on page 45). If the Fed manages to win a court fight on this point, the Treasury could buy it with US bonds.

The U.S. government claims to have 8,134 metric tonnes of gold in its reserves (an audit is needed). At 32,150 troy oz. per metric tonne, the US has 260.415 million troy ounces. Others say the US currently holds 261.5 mill. troy ounces, or 265 mill., but these figures are all close enough for this analysis. There is also a question as to the purity (fineness) of the US gold (debased or fake bars in storage, or gone on lease or loaned?). Only a proper audit will tell.

The Fed stopped publishing M3 in 2006 (claiming high expenses; I say to hide its growth!), but private sources put it at about $15 trillion worldwide in Feb-2012. If 100% of the M3 Fed Note dollars and bonds were made redeemable with our 260.415 million troy ounces of gold there would be 0.0000186 oz. per dollar (about 2 '100 thousandths'). This means 53,763 'gold-backed' Fed Note dollars would be redeemable for one troy ounce of gold. This implies a 97% drop in the dollar's current value versus today's about $1,750 per oz.; a 'gold value' ratio of about 34:1, to be known as the **'Conversion Factor'**. Some suggest we repudiate all federal debt, but this would be immoral (of course other nations –Russia, Argentina, etc.- have done it without legal backlash). The dreaded day of reckoning! But this issue fades as all nations convert to gold money (they must or no sellers will take their trash fiat 'money' once the US dollar is redeemable) and there is no 'price' for gold, just its weight.

It remains to be learned just how many 'Fed Note' dollars there are, and how much gold we have. On Aug. 25, 2010, former Rep. Ron Paul (R-TX) explained why we need to audit and inspect U.S. gold reserves in the Ft. Knox and the New York Fed vaults, and whether some has been secretly removed, leased, loaned, or some bars replaced by gold-plated base metal

Once the legal tender laws are repealed;
a. No additional units (physical or electronic, including new credit) of the old 'Fed Note' money will be issued. The free market will provide new money as needed; if the Fed isn't required to stop creating new money at first – due to politics, etc.- the new private money should proceed in parallel; let the best money win!,
b. Holders of old 'Fed Note' physical money would be required to convert it to new private money within two years of private money becoming legal,
c. The government must accept payments by 'new private money' if the issuing firm's reserves are at least forty percent, and have been verified to the public and gov't, and
d. Federal and State governments can issue new gold money, but it would have no privileges over private issues.

Step 4. To implement the new monetary system, I propose that Congress create the **'Currency Act of 2017'.** No government 'commission' is needed to ponder whether a gold standard is needed (unless forced for political reasons!). The Act should:
a) Incorporate the ideas and requirements in 'Redick's Four Monetary Rules' and this 'Five Step Plan',
b) Set the weight and fineness of gold that the existing Fed Notes and coins (physical, bond, or digital) will represent. This will involve debate as to % reserves and how many USD - M1, M3? - are covered, and the effective date. I suggest 100% of M3 and activation of the new system within 3 to 6 mo. after the Act is passed. Using M1 (or repudiating all debt) would have a lower inflationary impact on the dollar's value (more gold per dollar), but leave savings accounts, and domestic and foreign bond owners, with worthless paper, which amounts to default,

104

repudiation, and theft! Reserves of 40% for time deposits (savings) might be enough to avoid redemption 'runs' that would destroy the new system, but it is better to be on the safe side. A 'run' could ruin the system, just as occurred in the 1960s, ending in Nixon 'closing the gold window' in Aug-1971.

c) Require that new money issued by the U.S. Treasury (no Fed issues) be labeled only by weight and purity of gold (no 'name' or religious content) and made available on the day the new system is effective. All government transactions (fees, payments, taxes, Soc. Sec., bond principal, etc.) would be denominated by weight of gold. This will foster public use of gold weight as the unit of account for pricing.

d) Include lessons from how other nations changed money,

e) Publicize the discussions leading to the definition of the Act so US citizens and firms, and other nations, are aware and can submit their ideas and make their conversion plans. I oppose multi-nation planning conferences; they would just cause delays and dilution of terms.

f) The Act should include a **'Conversion Factor'** (about equal to the ratio of gold price between the new and old systems; '34' per Step 3 above) to adjust values in existing agreements (bonds, wages, loans, mortgages, pensions, insurance, etc.), and set new values by weight of gold. Using lower reserves, or M1, would reduce this factor but increase risk of a 'redemption run'. Pricing for new transactions or agreements would be set in the free market, and using 'weight of gold' as pricing would be encouraged.

Step 5. Terminate Useless and Harmful Organizations:

A. Domestic: Abolish the unconstitutional GSEs such as Fannie, Freddie, Ginnie, and Sallie Mae, FHA, Pension Benefit Guaranty Corp (PBGC), FDIC, all TARP-Like projects, the Exchange Stabilization Fund (ESF), Export-Import Bank, USAID, NSA, CIA, NED, etc., etc. All of these are part of the government's counter-productive intervention in, and manipulation of, money, private business, banking, and the affairs of other nations. While at it, end all unconstitutional departments and agencies!

B. International: Terminate US membership in the IMF (and get our gold back), World Bank, CBGA, BIS, G-20, G-8, NATO, United Nations, NAFTA, CAFTA, GATT, WTO, and others. The gold and silver price 'fix' groups are dying a painful death due to corruption. Free trade and embassies are adequate for contact with other nations.

Status of Federal Actions for Plan #1
While a few Congresspersons have spoken in favor of 'Gold as Money', led by former Rep. Ron Paul of TX-14th district (in office January 3, 1997 – January 3, 2013, visit ronpaulinstitute.org), no progress has been made to implement it. I hope some legislators keep up the fight. As stated on p. 98, it may never be approved, so we need an alternative (Plan #2). Visit campaignforliberty.com, and Tenthamendmentcenter.com to see their work for sound money, and to end the Fed monopoly.

xxxxxxxxxxxxxxxxxxxxxxxxxxxxxx

Description of Plan #2: The 'Bottom-Up' Plan Led by the States
The long-term plan for all States is to enforce Article 1, Section 10 of the U.S. Constitution which states; 'No State shall make any Thing but gold or silver Coin a Tender in payment of debts'. This ties-in with Section 8 which gives the Federal government the power to; '..to Coin money, Regulate the value thereof...'

Status of State Actions for Plan #2
The States of AZ, NC, NV, OK, TX, UT, and WA have passed (or close to) bills that treat gold as money, rather

than a commodity, so that increases in value are not taxed. This is an important first step. It is said that 13 other states are considering action.

In addition, TX has approved, by HB483 in June, 2015, a gold depository that will support transactions in gold. TX has requested that their $861.4 mill. of bullion, now in HSBC Bank in New York City, be expatriated to the new TX depository. A firm has been selected to build and operate the depository. It is expected that other States will do the same.

Further changes will be shown in revisions of this book, and on my web site SaferInvesting.org (see far right tab 'New Money' on top of the Home page). To see my essays on this, and other topics, go to my archive at ActivistPost.com, scroll to bottom of Home page and select 'Contributors', then my name.

xxxxxxxxxxxxxxxx

Blank

A Review of Other Conversion Plans

The above plans are unique because they; a) cut all mandatory ties to government (mint licenses are optional, no legal tender laws), b) abolish the central bank, convert all existing money and bonds (M3) to 'gold backed' as a transition, and uses 'weight of gold' as the unit of account for all 'new' money. I offer more detail than any plans I am aware of. I hope somewhere Mises, Rothbard, and Hayek are smiling.

Former Rep. Ron Paul M.D. gives a general description of his free-market monetary system on pages 203 to 207 in his 2009 book 'End the Fed'. Key issues are; 1. End legal tender laws and allow private mints, 2. All money redeemable in gold, and 3. Termination of the Fed (of course!). He discusses how purchasing power of the gold money (when in fixed supply) rises as GDP grows (more demand for money). This is the Appreciation effect presented in this book (p. 93, 95, 97, 140), which shows there is always 'enough' gold!

On November 9, 2010, Dr. Richard Ebeling, Professor of Economics at Northwood University (Northwood.edu), posted the article **'A Return to the Gold Standard?'** in the Daily Bell (dailybell.com) which touts a free-market system. See more about Ebeling on pages 28 and 122.

In an article on May 18, 2011, Robert Wenzel (economicpolicyjournal.com) wrote: *'...The current supply of gold owned by the United Sates should be divided by the number of dollars (Some version of M1) and made fully redeemable to those holders.'* Thanks Bob!

Lewis Lehrman's book 'The True Gold Standard' of Aug-2011 (TheGoldStandardNow.org, or LehrmanInstitute.org), proposes conversion of the USD to gold, then gold settlements with all world currencies, so no formal reserve currency is needed. Unfortunately, he retains legal tender laws and the Fed (or an equivalent).

In his Nov-2011 speech at the 'Cato Monetary Conference' (Cato.org) in D.C., Prof. L. White, Ph.D (economics.gmu.edu) proposed that since our banks are only required (usually) to have 20% reserves to back deposits, we only need to have gold reserves to redeem 20 percent of M1. I support his plan to make gold weight the 'unit of account', but I prefer use of M3 (see Step 4-b above), and fear that such low reserves could induce a 'run' by dollar and bond holders to redeem for gold.

Nathan Lewis (see page 127) wants to use of gold with 'a system to adjust the supply of base money.'

In May, 2014 Steve Forbes and co-author Elizabeth Ames, issued their book 'Money'. They call it a 'Gold Standard for the 21st Century', for 'sound' money with stable value, but it is loaded with government intervention which; seeks a fixed price of gold, treats gold as 'backing' (not money), uses gold only as a 'measure' that is not wealth (so has no role as a 'store of value'), and avoids redemption of paper notes for gold. They retain the Fed to manage interest rates, run the discount window, manage the USD price of gold, and serve as lender of last resort. It is a very flawed plan, designed to serve 'big government', and Cato Inst. erred in lauding it in their June 19, 2014 Book Forum.

How Gold Reserves Will Affect Conversion

The gold 'per currency unit' (Gold/M1) shown in Table 3 below, and 'per person' in Table 4, will have an impact when a nation converts to gold as money.

Table 3: Gold Reserves vs $M1 & Forex*

Country	Gold (tonnes)	M1 (bn USD)	Gold/M1 (tonnes/bn)	Gold % of Forex
Kuwait	79.0	15.3	5.163	13.8
Swiss	1040.1	225.2	4.619	15.3
USA	8133.5	2133.8	3.812	76.6
Saudi Ar.	322.0	87.9	3.663	3.3
India	557.7	233.7	2.631	9.6
Russia	936.7	300.0	2.584	9.6
Indonesia	73.1	39.7	1.841	3.5
Mexico	100.1	94.7	1.057	4.1
S. Africa	93.7	124.9	0.750	13.8
Sweden	125.7	184.2	0.682	13.6
Denmark	66.5	134.6	0.494	4.1
Australia	79.9	182.8	0.437	9.5
Brazil	33.6	84.1	0.400	0.5
China	1054.1	4175.0	0.252	1.8
Japan	765.2	3253.6	0.235	3.5
UK	310.3	1780.0	0.174	17.6
S. Korea	14.4	405.6	0.036	0.7
Canada	3.4	189.0	0.018	0.3

* Forex' is bank 'foreign exchange' reserves of gold, foreign currency, and foreign bonds used for international transactions.
* Credits to marketoracle.co.uk and dollardaze.org for M1 data, and en.wikipedia.org/wiki/Gold_reserve (Dec-2010; gold $1,400 oz) for Forex %. Russian M1 is an estimate.
Will the gold leaders in Table 2 'feel rich', 'live high', and buy assets abroad from owners that need gold? For sure, the low-end nations will have new incentive to be productive and get gold by exports, redemption U.S. T-bills for gold, or sale of assets.

Strong nations that have low amounts of gold in their reserves usually hold the cash or interest-bearing securities of strong foreign nations instead. This includes China, Japan, S. Korea, and Canada, plus others. They can redeem, or use 'as if gold', USD denominated assets after the US converts. Update; 90% of Portugal's Forex is gold.

Table 4: Gold Reserves per Person

Country	Gold (tonnes)	Population (millions)	Troy Ounces per person
Switzerland	1,040	7.9	4.249
Lebanon	287	4.3	2.166
Germany	3,401	81.8	1.337
Italy	2,452	60.8	1.298
France	2,435	65.4	1.198
Netherlands	613	16.7	1.178
Portugal	383	10.6	1.166
Austria	280	8.4	1.069
USA	8,134	313.0	0.836
Singapore	127	5.2	0.788
Kuwait	79	2.8	0.901
Belgium	228	10.8	0.676
Sweden	126	9.5	0.428
Russia	937	143.0	0.210
UK	310	62.3	0.160
Japan	765	127.7	0.138
China	1,054	1,339.7	0.025
India	558	1,210.2	0.015
Canada	3.4	33.5	0.0038

U.S. owners of gold will enjoy a one-time increase in value (purchasing power) when the conversion occurs, but this will fade as prices are increased. The situation will be dynamic, with many unpredictable market and government variables, including: a) How much gold the US will own once an audit is done, and b) What M3 and the price of gold will be by the time the Act is approved.

Since the 1990's, Canada and the UK have chosen to hold interest-bearing bonds rather than gold. Canada went from

1,083 tonnes in 1985 to 3.4 in 2011. China and India, both persons and government, have been 52% of world buying since 2010. China's total for 3rd quarter 2011 was about 146 metric tonnes, compared to 120 for all of 2010 ! The Chinese government is expected to announce its gold holdings in 2014. It will be big!, and part of the 'backing' if the yuan becomes a reserve currency.

There may be a rush of foreign buyers using their 'now more valuable' gold to acquire bargains in the US. To avoid losses, US sellers will increase prices as appropriate, per Step 4, item f), above. The free market will adjust.

Fortunately, the amount of gold per dollar or person is not crucial in the long run. When we start a new system of pricing by weight of gold, the market will adjust, and we will grow from there. The same applies to all nations that also convert, and they all will, or Sellers won't accept their fake money!

Central banks have acquired more gold in recent years. They often scoff at the need for gold as a 'barbarous relic' but in fact fear it because a rising gold price means the currency value is dropping. Table 4 is a sample of five nations, and total world holdings for all central banks.

Table 5: History of Central Bank Gold Reserves (metric tonnes)

Year	USA	Germany	France	Switzerland	UK	World Total
1850	x	x	x	x	105	109
1875	87	43	337	x	154	1089
1900	603	211	544	29	199	3175
1925	5998	432	1201	59	1046	13892
1950	20279	0	588	1306	2543	31096
1975	8584	3658	3139	2588	654	31790
2000	8137	3701	3184	2590	715	30025
2011	8134	3401	2435	1040	310	30563

Source: World Gold Council, Research Study 23

Comments about Table 4:
1. USA had redemption exports after 1944 when nations converted Fed Notes to gold due to our monetary inflation,
2. The UK sold about 395 tonnes from July 1999 to March 2002, at an average price of about USD275 per ounce,
3. Central Banks have been net buyers since Jan-2010.
****

Most central banks engage in buying and selling to 'stabilize' the gold price (see US 'ESF' on page 45) to suit political goals. They scoff at gold, but show they believe it has fundamental market value since they keep it in their reserves (if they can afford to).

Of the 160,000 tonnes of gold mined in history, the world allocation is about 52% for jewelry (83,200 tonnes), 19% central banks (30,563 tonnes), 16% investment bars, and coins (25,600 tonnes),11% industry (17,437 tonnes), and 2% (3,200 tonnes) not accounted for. About 50,000 tonnes is estimated as yet unmined.

As the world moves to gold-as-money, names like 'Dollars' can be eliminated and 'weight' will rule as the unit of account! Since the U.S. has trillions of fiat 'dollars' in circulation worldwide, the market value of a USD for conversion (trade-in) purposes will be a small fraction of an ounce, as shown in 'Step 3' on page 102. This implies that a minimum dollar amount may be required for an owner to redeem representative money for physical gold, since the tiny physical size of gold per dollar would be a problem in handling and measuring. If it were not a secret as to how much gold the government has at Fort Knox, the IMF, and in Federal Reserve facilities, a better estimate could be made.

Conversion of fiat money to gold money needs planning to avoid panic and uncertainty among current owners of fake money. Thus my Five-Step plan allows the Federal Reserve Notes to be redeemable for gold right away (but no new ones created), and used in a two year transition period during which they must be exchanged for new notes or coins from any mint. Since the existing Fed Notes will immediately represent gold, there will be no panic among Fed Note owners to get rid of their Notes (i.e., no 'redemption run').

Once the new gold money is introduced, I predict all nations will soon follow in converting to their own gold money as their fake money is refused as payment by Sellers and Lenders. In this case, good money drives out bad; the reverse of Gresham's Law. This would end the justification by governments for money-control schemes that central banks, the IMF, and the BIS pursue worldwide, which always do more harm than good.

Key changes to expect, all based on free market reality, not laws or 'G-20 style' agreements:

1. The concept of a 'reserve currency' would no longer be needed because any gold-based money would be accepted in world trade, or for bank reserves, if there was confidence it could be redeemed for gold

2. When most nations convert to gold money, the concept of a 'price' for gold will vanish. The reverse will occur, as coins or notes are 'valued' in the weight and fineness of gold they contain or represent, and Sellers advertise 'prices' in grams (milli, micro?) or ounces of gold,

3. The foreign exchange business (Forex) with banks will wither and die as it becomes useless, as will government manipulation such as the U.S. 'ESF' (see page 45).

4. People like to give 'names' to money (Dollar, Franc, etc.), but these would be social terms and would not need to appear on the money (but weight of gold would), unless the minter chooses to do so. Weight of gold will be the unit of account.

5. Nations will convert to gold money on their own terms, as and when needed. There will be no need for grand conferences (G20, G100?) to set rules, although some 'Agreements' may occur, and then whither when the 'rules' become onerous and counterproductive.

6. There will be no 'weak' or 'strong' currencies or 'pegs', all of which were part of the manipulations in the past. Gold will be the great equalizer and honest broker. The games will be over (and most of the wars).

7. In the present system of constant inflation, borrowers have the advantage of repaying loans with depreciated (less value) money, but with gold as money (by weight) its value may increase during the term of the loan, thus giving the lender an advantage of being paid in a weight that is more valuable. I predict that loan terms will be developed to adjust for this, because both borrowers and lenders will demand it. The likelihood of **appreciation** will also be a positive incentive to save more, and borrow less.

Patrick Barron, an Adjunct Instructor in Austrian Economics at the University of Iowa (patrickbarron.blogspot.com), said it well in his May 16, 2009 essay 'The World Does Not Need a Reserve Currency':

*"Each country should set its own ratio of local currency to gold and settle all trades in the actual commodity. Then no country—not the U.S., not the European Community, not China, nor Japan—will be able to inflate its currency without destroying its ability to import goods. It will run out of gold for settlement purposes and be forced to deflate. No special governmental agreements are needed. Gold would settle just as checks settle today—by debiting and crediting each nation's gold accounts wherever they may be. Just as no business can operate with zero money—it is forced to economize—**no nation would be able to import continuously by papering the world with its currency, as the U.S. does today.** As the profligate nation's gold reserves dwindled, its ability to import would dry up; prices would drop, making its goods a bargain for export; its gold reserves would start to climb and all would be well."* I first read this in Jan-2012. It ties-in with my '**5. Fewer Jobs 'Off-Shored'** statement on page 119.

Summary: As painful as the transition to 'gold as money' may be for some people and nations, it is better than the chaotic hyperinflationary crash (with money values approaching zero) that is otherwise 99% likely to occur under our present worldwide fiat money, and central banking system. Since it is unlikely that Congress will vote to reduce their control and production of money, Plan #2 has a better chance of being implemented because the States like how it; a) ends the Federal monopoly (and thus control of many State projects), and b) avoids a monetary crash that will destroy the USA economy and culture.

XXXXXXXXXXXXXXX

Cryptocurrencies:

Computer-based currency has evolved in an effort by users to avoid the restrictions and depreciation of fiat money from governments and banks. 'Bitcoin' is a leader, with several more available. Jeff Berwick at DollarVigilante.com has been very active in reporting on this market (Newsletter@DollarVigilante.com). See his video seminars at; https://dollarvigilante.com/nationless-private-bank?cfid=139 . The seminar shows the status of ten crypto currencies. For info about a large exchange see Coinbase.com.

Cryptos have made spectacular gains in value since Bitcoin started in 1990. However, my view is that since the current demand for crypto currencies is based solely on problems with existing government fiat currencies, the demand for, and price of, cryptos will fall if; a) new commodity–based currencies appear, and b) abuse and fraud become part of crypto management (the Block Chain algorithm; a ledger) as it has with all non- commodity currency in the past. All cryptos are created and managed by human, and there lies the risk of abuse. Blockchains are also created by humans, and can be changed by them! For more info, visit http://www.investopedia.com/terms/b/blockchain.asp.

Chapter 5: The New Gold Money Era

The Challenges of Introducing Gold

Some will say that this plan for new money is too simplistic, and will not work in todays' complex world. I say they are wrong, because most of the complexity is created by government manipulation of their fake money, and those problems will end when fake money ends. Most (over 95%) of today's self-serving politicians and economists have bought the idea that; 1. the government must run the 'economy' and monetary system, 2. all financial activities must be tightly regulated to avoid abuse, and 3. there must be a central bank. Of course they are biased, because they want the jobs, grants, and perquisites that come with this approach, and have been so brainwashed in college and work that most of them can't imagine another way, and they are WRONG!

The new era will depend more on incentive than regulation Gold money in a free market is self-regulating. The heroin-upper effect of loose money will be gone (see Heroin Analogy on page 38). People operate differently when using limited funds, and without the perverse incentive of a bailout. A fake and excessive supply of money creates a pot of honey that breeds irresponsibility and bad ethics as people scramble to get more of it. Gold money puts a damper on this frenzy because governments can't create it out of thin-air, short of reducing reserves for paper 'representative' money, which has its limits too.

What will other nations do? The people, merchants, and governments will prefer the new gold money, and it will prompt conversions to gold in other nations since their fake money will soon be rejected as payment by sellers and lenders worldwide.

Thus, I see no long-term 'downside' to the future with gold as money. Of course there will be hardships during the conversion, but the alternative of a hyperinflation depression is worse.

Bullion Coins and Private Medallions

As a partial step toward using precious metal coins again, the 1933 law that prohibited private ownership of gold coins and bullion (numismatic coins and jewelry were allowed) was repealed in 1975. In 1985, Pres. Reagan approved the 'Gold Bullion Coin Act of 1985' and 'Public Law 99-61' for silver, to create the 'Eagle' series. Both coins were soon popular worldwide. Since then the US Mint (http://www.usmint.gov/) has issued a variety of gold, silver, and platinum bullion coins. As shown in Table 5, their face values are far below their market value, and thus, though they are legal tender, are not used in commerce (somewhere a bureaucrat is laughing!). They are sold at 'spot price' for the metal content, plus fees for production and profit ('seniorage'). However, one businessman paid his employees with $5 gold Eagles (see P. 119) and they filed their income taxes based on the low face value. The IRS sued but gave up due to a hung jury. Many other nations offer bullion coins.

Although some bullion coins are legal tender, due to low face values they are all viewed as investments, and are not used as money. A bonus is that they posture the owners to use them at bullion value if Congress ever repeals the legal tender laws and allows use of private mints and coins. See former Rep. Ron Paul's HR-4248. They could also come into use if we have a chaotic economic crash and people start using gold, and other commodities, as money. Many US dealers sell the bullion, medallions, numismatic coins, and bars issued by various countries and private mints. For your convenience (not a recommendation), examples are:

1. Precious Metal Dealers; InvestmentRarities.com, SchiffGold.com, caminocompany.com, monex.com, , MoneyMetals.com, blanchardonline.com, goldmoney.com , Apmex.com, HardAssetsAlliance.com, and more.

2. Private Mints; nwtmint.com, CoinsForAnything.com, and medalcraft.com. Use an Internet search engine (Google, etc.) to find more. Many private 'mints' make precious metal medallions as commemorative pieces for private use (jewelry, keepsakes, etc.). The mints have die-makers (craftsmen) and presses so can quickly design and produce new pieces with any imprint.

3. Foreign Currencies and Stock: EuroPacific Capital (EuroPac.net) is a broker that offers purchase of stock and funds denominated in foreign currencies. Everbank (Everbank.com) is a bank that offers savings accounts in foreign currencies. Ron Holland, www.bfi-consulting.com , is an author (TheDailyBell.com) and advises investors for global diversification outside U.S. markets and the dollar. Some of the most popular government-issued gold coins are shown in Table 5. See P. 18 for more on coins.

Table 6:   Bullion Coins

Country	Name	Metal	Sizes (troy oz.)	Face Values ($)
USA	Eagle	0.9167 Gold	1,1/2, 1/4, 1/10	$50, 25, 10, 5
USA	Silver Eagle	0.9999 Silver	1	$1
Canada	Mapleleaf	0.9999 Gold	1,1/2, 1/4, 1/10	C$20,10,5,1
So. Africa	Krugerrand	0.9167 Gold	1, 1/2, 1/4, 1/10	no FV
P. R. China	Panda	0.9999 Gold	1, 1/2, 1/4, 1/10	no FV

(24 carat = 0.9999 pure gold   22 carat = 0.9167 pure)

In addition to survival gear (see page 81), a prudent person will own an ample supply of small bullion gold coins (1/4 and 1/10 oz), or old legal tender silver coins (pre-1965 US dollars, quarters and dimes). People will soon learn that they have 0.72 oz silver content per dollar (0.18 for quarter, 0.072 for dime), for use as money if it becomes legal to trade at the bullion value (or a black market will start). If the value of gold and silver soar after the crash, these will be useable sizes with strong purchasing power, but even lower value coins will be needed.

Benefits of a Gold-Money World

In summary, we can expect the following benefits when the new gold money becomes legal:

1. More Peace: Wars are very expensive. The absence of an unlimited supply of fake money will inhibit the starting of wars; Diplomacy will be used instead. Imperialistic aggressors will have trouble getting funded.

2. More Prosperity: Gold money will increase in value (purchasing power) if percent economic growth exceeds the percent addition of newly mined gold. Savings will be rewarded, more money value will be available for investments, and managers can plan better.

3. Less Government: Governments need money to grow. Taxation has its limits, and in the absence of the unlimited supply of fake money, government programs, staffing, and spending will be limited. There will be less intervention in, and control of, our lives and work. More Liberty, Peace, and Prosperity will be the dividends.

4. Fewer and Smaller Business Cycles and Depressions: The 'highs' of major business cycles are caused by bad investments due to excessive availability of money (credit and currency); too many new dollars chasing a limited number of deals, many of which are high risk. The incentive is to 'do something' with the excessive money. When the pool of money is reduced (Fed cutbacks) the frenzy drops like a rock. With a limited supply of real gold money, any frenzies would soon run out of money to feed them, and the cycles would be small or none.

5. Fewer Jobs 'Off-Shored': Due major increase in US wage and benefit costs after WW2, starting in the '80s, factories were built in other nations where costs are lower (first Mexico, then China, India, etc.) and the jobs moved out of the US! The same applies to software since the '90s. In addition, there is no limit to how much a country can import when it issues the world's reserve currency and can make it out of thin air. That's why our imports have soared since 1971 (when Nixon ended the dollar's tie to gold), and many of our factories have shut down. With gold as money, the importers run out of money, and local producers get the business. This is one of the self-regulating aspects of gold. (above '5.' was first published in Jan-2010)

6. Fewer Sovereign Defaults and No Currency Devaluations: In the past, many nations have defaulted (stopped payments) on some or all of their debt when they became overburdened, and then devalued (reduced face value) their currency to increase exports (lower prices). This robs lenders, and holders of the currency, but lets the nation enjoy a 'fresh-start', hopefully with reduced government spending and fewer anti-business laws. Argentina in 2002 is a recent example. When gold is money, the devalue option ends, which should give politicians and citizens incentive to keep their laws and economy more competitive. This new attitude will also reduce the excessive spending that leads to defaults. (above '6.' first published in Nov-2011).

****

We can enjoy these benefits, and avoid a crash of our economy, currency and lifestyle if we implement this plan for gold money. If we crash, meaning severe reduction in economic activity (depression), and 50% to 90% loss of purchasing power of the US dollar, we will need to rebuild from the 'ashes'. This can be viewed as an opportunity for the people to spontaneously start using gold as money. They will see its benefits, and demand to keep it! The laws can follow. Politicians will be desperate to keep their jobs so will cooperate to pass and repeal laws as needed; otherwise they will be fired and replaced.

It will require something like the above 'crash' circumstances, and a people-led Monetary Revolution, to take back our government from the self-serving career politicians, empire-building warmongers (neocons), and banksters.

Will you help? A key purpose of this book is to build support for the conversion to gold, and be ready to act when the right time comes to push changes through Congress. In the meantime, we should be working to elect like-minded people to Congress, and educating those already there.

Until the above changes are made, we need to defend ourselves against financial losses. To see my ideas, look at chapter 5 'Investment Strategy' in my book **'How to Protect and Grow Your Wealth'.** The book is available at Amazon.com.. Contact me at RedickD@aol.com

Thanks for your interest and support,
Dave Redick

Part 2:
Contents: 1. Authors, p. 125, 2. Appendix, p. 133, 3. Glossary, p. 139, 4. Dave's Bio, p. 146.

1. Authors, Books, and Sources:
Index: A. Authors-P.125, B. Books-P.130, C. Organizations-P.132, D. Internet Sites-P.132

A. Authors Noted in this Book. (alpha order)

1. Douglas R. Casey: In his book **'Crisis Investing'**, 1979, Doug predicted a major depression due to government intervention. It came in 2008! He; 1) Is an independent thinker, with 'on the ground' business experience (not biased by academic rules and vanity), 2) Supports liberty, the gold standard, and limited government as the path to peace and prosperity, and 3) Has written these books about investing and government; His new book **'Totally Incorrect"**, 2012, with L. James and T. Coxon, is an unabashed treatise for libertarianism and free-market capitalism; **'Crisis Investing'**, 1995; and **'The International Man'** 1979, with H. Schulz. See his articles: 1) Feb-2012 about war, oil, gov't, and gold at: lewrockwell.com/casey/casey108, 2) Mar-2012, 'The Ascendence of Sociopaths in US Governance' lewrockwell.com/casey/casey112, and 3) Nov-2012 'The America That Was – Now the United (Police) State of America'. His archives are at; lewrockwell.com/casey/casey-arch, and caseyresearch.com/cdd/archives.

2. Donlan. Thomas G.: He joined Barron's as a reporter 1979, and became its editorial page editor in 1992 (Barrons.com). His books are; "*Supertech*," 1991, "*Don't Count On It*," 1994, and "*A World of Wealth: How Capitalism Turns Profit into Progress*," in 2008. These books present his case on a range of topics. In his columns, he writes about the power of capitalism and how free markets and free-enterprise offer the best solutions to create more liberty, peace, prosperity, justice, and morality in a nation or society.

3. Ebeling, Richard, Ph.D., (1950-): He received his B.A. degree in economics from California State University, Sacramento, his M.A. degree in economics from Rutgers University, and a Ph.D. in economics from Middlesex University in London, UK. He was president of the Foundation for Economic Education (FEE) from 2003 to 2008, and has written and edited numerous books and articles, including the three-volume *Selected Writings of Ludwig von Mises* (Liberty Fund), recovered from Russia. His most recent works are *Political Economy, Public Policy, and Monetary Economics: Ludwig von Mises and the Austrian Tradition,* (2010), and *Austrian Economics and the Political Economy of Freedom,* (2003). More on page 28.

4. Edwards, Michael: After graduating from Rutgers University, Michael Edwards began his career as a technical writer and editor operating freelance for trade magazines and books in a variety of areas. In early 2010, Michael co-founded ActivistPost.com, a blog where his own writings appear, along with co-founder, Eric Blair, as well as many contributors. They post new articles daily on a broad range of issues which challenge the diluted, biased, and often false info the political 'establishment' and Main Stream Media offer.

5. F. William Engdahl: His writing and research bridges the disciplines of economics, politics, and the less known field of geopolitics. His books on oil and geopolitics are; **'A Century of War: Anglo-American Politics and the New World Order'**, and **'Full Spectrum Dominance: Totalitarian Democracy in the New World Order**, which deals with the Pentagon agenda of global hegemony in the post-Cold War era. He is a writer and consulting economist and teaches at the University of Applied Sciences, Wiesbaden, Germany. His website is, www.engdahl.oilgeopolitics.net

6. Fekete, Antal, Ph.D.: He is a mathematician, monetary scientist and educator. He is a proponent of the gold standard and a critic of the current monetary system. Go to the Home page of www.professorfekete.com to see 'Remobilize Gold to Save the World Economy', and other writings. He has been criticized for his emphasis on 'real bills'.

7. Hayek, Frederick A., Ph.D.: Nobel Laureate.
See; 'Denationalization of Money: The Argument Refined', 1976, which puts forth the case to; 1) end the government monopoly on money creation, 2) let anyone create money, and 3) let the free market determine which type of money is used.

8. Laffer Ph.D., Arthur: While on the Reagan staff in the 1980s he was one of the creators of Supply-Side Economics and the Laffer Curve, which shows the tradeoff between tax rates and revenues. His books include 'End of Prosperity', and most recently 'Return to Prosperity'. He earned an MBA and Ph.D. in economics from Stanford University. See www.laffercenter.com.

9. Lehrman, Lewis: An ardent promoter of the benefits of the gold standard for over thirty years, he co-chaired Reagan's 'U.S. Gold Commission' with Dr. Ron Paul in 1981, and co-authored their Minority Report, 'The Case for Gold' in 1982. His new book 'The True Gold Standard' (Aug-2011, published by LehrmanInstitute.org) is his latest effort.

10. Miller, Donald W., Jr., M.D.: He is a cardiac surgeon and Professor of Surgery at the University of Washington in Seattle, and writes on politics, health and medicine. For a start, see his excellent 'A Fourteen Point Plan for a Post-Wilsonian America' at http://www.lewrockwell.com/orig2/miller2.html, and his archives at www.lewrockwell.com. His web site is www.donaldmiller.com.

11. Mises S.J.D., Ludwig von: As the leading scholar of the 'Austrian School' of economics, Mises has written many books, led by **'Human Action'** (1949), **'Socialism'** (1922), and **'The Theory of Money and Credit'** (1912). See more at www.mises.org.

12. **Paul, Rep. Ron, MD (R-TX, retired):** He wrote **'The Revolution: A Manifesto'** in Apr-2008, **'End the Fed'** in Sep-2009, and **'The Case for Gold'**, with L. Lehrman, in 1982. A

Republican candidate for President in the 2008 and 2012 primaries. Dr. Paul says we have been lied-to, robbed and abused by our own government. He retired from Congress in Jan-2013. On April 17, 2013 Dr. Paul announced creation of his 'Institute for Peace and Prosperity', with a mission to educate and advocate for a peaceful foreign policy and the protection of civil liberties at home. (ronpaulinstitute.org). Also visit campaignforliberty.com, and dailypaul.com.

13. Quinn, James: He is Senior Director of Strategic Planning for a major university, and author of a series of essays on world financial affairs. For more, go to http://seekingalpha.com/author/james-quinn , and his main site; http://www.theburningplatform.com/

14. James Rickards is an investment banker, speaker, and author of; 1) 'Currency Wars: The Making of the Next Global Crisis', Nov-2012. He shows that currency wars are one of the most destructive and feared outcomes in international economics, and 2) 'The End of Money', April-2014. More at jimrickards.blogspot.com

15. Roberts Ph.D., Paul Craig; An Economist and author of eight books and many articles on economics and politics; all based on fact and logic, and seeking the truth. He holds a Ph.D. from the University of Virginia. He a former associate editor of the Wall Street Journal, a former Assistant Secretary of the U.S. Treasury with Reagan. See his site paulcraigroberts.org (click on 'Articles' to see 'Assault on Gold', April-2013), and his full story at http://en.wikipedia.org/wiki/Paul_Craig_Roberts.

16. Rothbard, Murray, Ph.D., 1926-1995, was a prominent economist of the Austrian school, Professor, and prolific author. See 'What has the Government Done to our Money?', 1964, 'Origins of the Federal Reserve', 'The Mystery of Banking', 1983, and **'The Case for the 100% Gold Dollar'**, 1962, at http://www.lewrockwell.com/rothbard/rothbard207.html, and more at http://www.mises.org/money.asp

17. Salerno Ph.D., Joseph, is a professor of economics at Pace University and chair of the economics graduate program. He is also a senior faculty member of the Mises Institute, for which he frequently lectures and writes about monetary policy and banking.

18. Schiff, Peter, is President of Euro Pacific Capital, and author of 'The Real Crash' (2012), 'The Little Book of Bull Moves in Bear Markets' (2008, 2010) and 'Crash Proof: How to Profit from the Coming Economic Collapse' (2009). See europac.net, and archives at www.lewrockwell.com/schiff/schiff-arch.

19. Selgin Ph.D., George, is an economic historian whose research has convinced him that minimal governmental intervention in financial matters and that markets with fewer regulations are more robust and better at generating wealth and economic development. A prolific author, he now teaches economics and monetary subjects at Terry School of Business, University of Georgia, Athens. Starting in Sep-2014, he will run the new **'Center for Monetary Studies'** at Cato Inst. in DC.

20. Wenzel, Robert: A financial consultant and author of economicpolicyjournal.com, he writes with an Austrian perspective on economics, and keeps us informed on world activity and his opinions about it. He promotes sound money, such as the gold standard, but opposes government meddling as done by central banks.

21. White Ph.D., Lawrence H. (economics.gmu.edu) is author of 'The Theory of Monetary Institutions' (1999), 'Free Banking in Britain' (2nd ed., 1995), 'Competition and Currency' (1989), and other volumes. He specializes in banking and money.

22. Woods Jr., Ph.D., Thomas E.: He is a historian with focus on government, economics, and law. Of his eleven books, those that apply most here are 'Rollback' (2011) and 'Meltdown' (2009).

B. Books:

1. 'The Blowback Triology', a trilogy by Chalmers Johnson, 1931-2010, (Blowback-2000, Sorrows of Empire-2004, Nemesis-2007), plus Dismantling the Empire-2010. Johnson shows how our meddling, and expensive, foreign policy does harm'

2. 'The Coming Collapse of the Dollar and How to Profit from It', Dec-2004 (2008), by James Turk and John Rubino. They describe how monetary systems have long been abused by governments. See; fgmr.com, goldmoney.com (buy and store precious metals), www.dollarcollapse.com, and www.cmre.org

3. 'The Creature from Jekyll Island: A Second Look at the Federal Reserve', Edition #1,1994; #5, 2010, by G. Edward Griffin (realityzone.com and freedomforceinternational.org). He reveals the sinister origins and self-serving goals of the bankers who started the Fed, and publishes the FFI newsletter.

4. 'Empire of Debt', 2006, by W. Bonner and A. Wiggins. It addresses how excessive national debt and spending can drastically reduce the value of the U.S. dollar, and cause a major depression.

5. 'The Great Reckoning: How the world will change in the depression of the 1990s', 1991, by J. Davidson and Lord R. Mogg. They warn of economic collapse of the US due to overspending and Empire-style foreign policy.

6. a) **'Index of Economic Freedom'**, annual since 1994, The Heritage Foundation, charts economic success vs. freedom; www.heritage.org/research/features/index/ and b**) Economic Freedom of the World**: Annual report by Cato Institute, http://www.cato.org/pubs/

7. 'A Nation of Sheep', 1961, by William Lederer (also 'The Ugly American'), is about how Americans accept abuse by the government without complaint, as long as the 'good times roll'.

8. **'A Nation of Sheep'**, 2007, by Andrew Napolitano, (also 'Constitutional Chaos' and 'Lies the Government Told You'), is about how Americans accept abuse by the government without complaint or curiosity, as long as the 'good times roll'.

9. 'Gold, The Once and Future Money', 2007. by Nathan Lewis. An economist by trade, Lewis refers to 'good money' as the 'cornerstone of good government', and promotes the gold standard as the best system. www.newworldeconomics.com

10. 'Trends 2000', 1997, by Gerald Celente. A 'futures analyst', he tells how to prepare and profit from changes in the 21st century. Visit www.trendsresearch.com

11. Older Books that Gave Warning and Good Advice

a. 'The Law', 1850, by F. Bastiat. With his perspective of the French Revolution, he explains the fallacies of Socialism and how it must degenerate into Communism.

b. 'The True Believer', 1951, by Eric Hoffer, a book which shows how people join a group or mass to bring a sense 'belonging' or 'superiority'.

c. 'Capitalism: The Unknown Ideal', 1967, by Ayn Rand. Discusses both the productive and moral aspects of Capitalism. Review by Alan Greenspan (before joining the Fed banksters)

d. 'None Dare Call It Conspiracy', 1972, Gary Allen with Larry Abraham. Probes the secret dealings of bankers, industrialists, and politicians to distort US policy and money for their own gain.

e. 'A Time for Truth', 1979, by William Simon. Bill warned us of the damage being caused by excessive spending, taxes, and the debasement of our currency.

f. 'An American Renaissance', 1979, by Rep. Jack Kemp. Jack sent an upbeat message on how less government spending and lower taxes would produce more growth, all based on his support of Austrian economics.

g. 'Restoring the American Dream', 1979, by Robert Ringer. Robert warned us of a trend in the US to expect a 'free lunch', and how we can reverse the trend.

C. Organizations: Free-market and limited government oriented essays, books, blogs, meetings, and courses.
1. The Cato Institute: www.cato.org
2. The Independent Institute: www.independent.org
3. The Ludwig von Mises Institute: Daily essays are at www.LewRockwell.com, plus books and articles at mises.org.
4. Reason Foundation: A magazine and www.reason.org
5. Foundation for Economic Education: www.Fee.org

D. Internet Sites:

1. For more on money and gold, visit: ,
en.wikipedia.org/wiki/Money_supply, zerohedge.com, goldstandardinstitute.net, gold.org, mises.org/freemarket_detail.aspx?control=483, kitco.com, history.com/minisites/money/viewPage?pageId=52498, DollarCollapse.com, goldmoney.com, cmre.org, fgmr.com, en.wikipedia.org/wiki/History_of_money,goldismoney.info, measuringworth.com, MoneyWatch.com, shadowstats.com, xat.org/xat/moneyhistory, 321Gold.com, USDebtClock.org, GATA.org, .

2. General Web Sites about Government & Economics: See a flow of essays from; LewRockwell.com, Activistpost.com, WindRockWealth.com, Antiwar.com, FFF.org, Truthdig.com, Alternet.org, VDare.com, reason.org, pacificreasearch.org, freedomforceinternational.org, independent.org, pacificlegal.org, cato.org, online.barrons.com, garynorth.com, LP.org, dailyreckoning.com, pgpf.org, mises.org, shadowstats.com, economicpolicyjournal.com, informationclearinghouse.info, a2zPublications.com, trendsresearch.com, freedomworks.com, campaignforliberty.org

2. Appendices:

Appendix 1:

Go to the Home page of www.professorfekete.com to see '**Remobilize Gold to Save the World Economy'**, by Dr. Antal Fekete. Here is an excerpt: *'The debt crisis of 2008 was a dress rehearsal. It gave the world a foretaste.* This crisis is a gold crisis. *It is a crisis indicating the threat of a shortage of the ultimate extinguisher of debt, without which our runaway debt tower is doomed. When it topples, it will bury the world economy under the rubble, as the Twin Towers buried the people working inside in 2001.'* Dr. Fekete is a mathematician, monetary scientist and educator. He is a proponent of the gold standard and a critic of the current monetary system. Also see his '**Proposed Parallel Gold-Coin Standard to the Federal Reserve System'** at http://www.afr.org/antal.html .

Appendix 2:

(Note: This Op-Ed is included because all of the wars shown below were financed by fake money, Dave)

Published Mon. Sep. 10, 2007 in the Wisconsin State Journal (www.madison.com), a regional daily newspaper based in Madison, and ActivistPost.com as '13 Lies…' (on 15Dec2010, click on 'Contributors' then scroll down to 'original archives', by year & month).

'Wars and the Lies That Start Them'

By David Redick

Our presidents, and their complicit henchmen, have lied us into every war since the revolution in 1776.

Their real reasons have not been legal, constitutional, or politically acceptable, so they invent one or more false reasons that they can "sell " to the people.

Sadly, most people believe the lies, and proudly support them as "wars for defense. " They can't imagine that our leaders would be so evil as to spend the lives of our troops to gain their hidden political and economic goals for Empire-USA.

The secret plan of Bush and his gang was to: 1) Take over all oil in the Middle East so we don 't have to share it with China and India, 2) Land for bases, 3) Evict China from Eastern Europe and Africa, and 3) Defend Israel at any cost. Control of oil was the hidden reason for the Balkans, Afghan, and Iraq wars.

Iran is their next target.

The war drums are beating in Washington to justify bombing Iran, so this is a good time to consider whether our leaders are lying again. Here are the facts on how we got into a few major wars. Each one could be a book, so please forgive the brevity.

War of 1812 (Madison, 1812)

Lies: In 1812, Congress declared war on England based primarily on their kidnapping ("impressment ") of our sailors at sea. Truth: To drive England out of North America and get southern land. The war started with our invasion of Canada, at Detroit. We burned their Parliament buildings in York (now Toronto), so they burned DC ! The 'Star Spangled Banner' was written when British boats shelled Baltimore Harbor.

Mexican-American War (Polk, 1845)

Lies: Fight to defend our Texas border with Mexico. Truth: We invaded to expand, and took the northern half of Mexico, now our entire Southwest region.

Civil War (Lincoln, 1865)

Lies: Fight to end slavery and preserve the union. Truth: The South seceded due to economic abuse by the North. Slavery was ended later (but only in Southern states).

Spanish-American War (McKinley, 1898)

Lies: Spain blew-up the U.S. battleship Maine in Cuba 's Havana harbor. Truth: The accidental explosion was used to invade Cuba, and the Philippines (for a Pacific port).

World War I (Wilson, 1917)

Lies: Join Europe to "Make the World Safe for Democracy. " Truth: Wilson was convinced to join by U.S. and European industrialists.

World War II (FDR, 1941)

Lies: Defend the United States from unprovoked attacks by Japan. Truth: FDR wanted be sure Germany didn't win and become a world power, and also preserve our Far East oil and industrial sources and markets, so he poked Japan until he got his "incident."

Korean War (Truman, 1950)

Lies: Defend America. Truth: Truman and the generals wanted a reason to have troops in the Far East area of our Empire.

Vietnam War (Kennedy, 1955)

Lies: Johnson said Vietnam attacked our ships in the Gulf of Tonkin. Truth: The United States didn't want to lose the southeast Asia region, and its oil, to China.

Gulf War (Bush-41, 1990)

Lies: To defend Kuwait from Iraq. Truth: Saddam was a threat to Israel, and we wanted his oil.

Balkans (Clinton, 1998)

Lies: Prevent Serb killing of Bosnians. Truth: Get the Chinese out of Eastern Europe and Caspian Sea areas so they couldn't get control of the oil.

Afghanistan (Bush-43, 2001)

Lies: The Taliban were hiding Osama. Truth: To access the east of Caspian oil region by building a gas/oil pipeline from Turkmenistan, thru Afghan, to a warm water port near Karachi.

Iraq (Bush-43, 2003)

Lies: Stop use of WMDs, or bring democracy. Truth: Oil, defense of Israel, land for permanent bases and restore oil sales in the U. S. dollar.

Possible Iran War

Lies: They almost have an atom bomb. Truth: Oil, end sales in gold, and defense of Israel.

Fight the Bush gang to stop their plans for war against Iran.

****

Redick is President of www.SaferInvesting.org

Appendix 3:

This article below was published as the 'Guest Column' on Jan. 29, 2008 by the Wisconsin State Journal, a regional daily newspaper based in Madison, WI (www.madison.com), by David Redick.

'Fake Money: Cause of Wars, Depressions' .

On Jan. 22, 2008, the Federal Reserve System issued an interest rate cut to "rescue the economy. " This shows how counterproductive government "management " of the economy is.

It creates problems with too much easy money (mortgages), and then tries to solve them with more of the same (a "stimulus " package). The analogy is that easy money is like a heroin high, and recessions are like withdrawal. In each case, it is better to avoid the fake highs and let the free market work.

Our monetary system is very important because it affects government policy so much.

Our leaders in Congress want an unlimited supply of that money so they can continue to give handouts to voters and fund wars for empire, such as Iraq.

Since only the federal government can create money, we see an increase in the number of state projects funded by Washington and more pork from the Capitol.

You won 't read the following analysis in the newspapers or in a college economics course. Most politicians, business leaders and professors like the current system of fake money, because their jobs, grants, and social lives depend on it.

Thus they ridicule the idea of real money (redeemable for gold, by any person, on demand) as old-fashioned.

However, history and logic show us that the use of real money, not subject to manipulation by government, is fundamental to the long-term success and survival of a nation.

Conversely, all failing nations in history have resorted to debasement of their currency, using worthless paper and less-precious metal in coins, to fund their excessive spending. Fake paper money, managed by the Federal Reserve, is what allows the massive spending and debt for wars and domestic pork and welfare that have brought the United States to the brink of economic collapse.

The Fed is a private bank created in 1913, which was granted authority to produce our currency and manage our monetary system. Its mission to bring stability and maintain the dollar's value has been a failure. The U.S. dollar has lost 95 percent of its purchasing power since 1913, and 40 percent against the Euro since 2001.

The key reason to allow redeemability of paper 'representative' money to a commodity is to limit excessive expansion of the money supply. The commodity could be wheat, iron, diamonds, or pearls, but gold works best for many practical reasons. Politicians hate real money because it limits their spending.

The United States is bankrupt due to excessive debt, spending and future obligations, with no cure in sight. Those countries that own a lot of U.S. dollars can't afford to dump them as their value declines due to fear of starting worldwide panic selling.

But history shows us that something always triggers panic selling and a crash. This crash could reduce the value of the U.S. dollar by 50 percent or more in a few days, and start a worldwide depression. Sadly, very few people understand or care about currency issues. Instead, they prefer our version of Roman bread and circuses as we crash.

Redick of Madison is President of www.SaferInvesting.org.

Appendix 4: **The Phases of Empire**

This analysis explains why all empires, and 'Imperial Style' governments, in history have failed, and why our 'Empire-USA' faces the same fate. For more, visit;
http://www.activistpost.com/2010/08/phases-of-empire.html

3. Dave's Glossary:

1. Central Bank: Whether private or owned by the government, a central bank usually has certain government-bestowed duties and privileges such as; a) The sole right to issue currency and market government securities, b) Allowed to operate in almost total secrecy to supposedly avoid political influence, c) Set interest rates, d) Buy government securities to fund government expenses, e) Stabilize the value of the currency and keep unemployment low (these may be fake duties, but sound good!), f) Serves as the 'Lender of Last Resort' to banks short of cash (a sweet deal for casino bankers!), and g) other acts. The CB typically works closely with the Treasury Department, and key managers may be appointed by the government. In the U.S., it is the Federal Reserve System.

2. Deflation: The opposite of Monetary Inflation; a reduction in the money supply, and an increase in purchasing power of each money unit, thus lower prices. Not to be confused with 'depression'.

3. Depression: Any economic downturn where real GDP (Gross Domestic product) declines by more than 10 percent. Also; Two or more quarters of reduced GDP. A **recession** is an economic downturn that is less severe.

4. Economics: (Types, alpha order)

a. 'Austrian School' of economic thought (Hayek, von Mises, Rothbard), emphasizes the spontaneous organizing power of free market pricing, decisions by individuals, gold as money, and little or no government management or stimulation of the economy.

b. Capitalism - An 'economic system' based on private ownership, free enterprise, and minimal regulation. It offers more than economic results. **It is a moral system** that depends on willing buyers and sellers within the rule of law, not coercion and control by others. It has been re-defined as a mean, self-centered, you're on your own, 'social system' by those who prefer Socialism (sharing by force, causing a more equal but lower standard of living for all). The U.S. now has **'Crony Capitalism'**, a damaging distortion where firms and people get favors from government (often in exchange for campaign donations!).

c. Communism: The government owns all housing, agriculture, industry and transportation (almost everything but the clothes on your back). The government tells you where to live, go to college (if any), and where to work.

d. Fascism allows private ownership of businesses, but there is extensive government control and preeminence.

e. 'Keynesian Theory' (started by J. M. Keynes and now used by Krugman, Samuelson, Stiglitz, Bernanke) depends on massive use of government fiscal (spending) and monetary (interest rates, money supply) policy trying to create prosperity or avoid and end depressions. History and logic show the Keynes approach is unsustainable and never works for more than a year or two (longer if supported by natural resources; oil, timber, mining, etc.).

f. Monetarism: An approach identified with the 'Chicago School of economics led by Prof. Milton Friedman Ph.D. of the University of Chicago. It emphasizes management of the money supply by the Fed to control inflation and GDP growth. Most Monetarists dislike the gold standard as 'too inflexible' in changing the money supply, except by mining more gold or silver. They are wrong because they ignore how the purchasing power of gold increases (appreciates) with more demand. Thus, there is always 'enough'.

g. Socialism: Most of the means of production and trade (factories, railroads, etc) are owned by the government, which sets pricing, product types, etc. The government controls most wages, with an emphasis on 'fairness', need, and 'hours worked', rather than value of the service performed. High, and steeply progressive, taxes support a 'single-payer health system and pension plan

h. 'Supply Side' economics: This school of thought emphasizes increasing incentive to invest by reductions in; **a.** capital gains and income taxes (focusing on lower marginal rates), and **b.** regulation. These should be the first steps to revive a troubled economy because they have the lasting effect of stimulating action by producers and investors. "Supply Side' was originated by economists P. C. Roberts Ph.D., Robert Mundell Ph.D., and Arthur Laffer Ph.D., and politicians Pres. Ronald Reagan and Rep. Jack Kemp in the 1980s.

5. Fiat Money: Fiat (by decree) money is worth whatever the government says it is (face value), although the material of which it is made may have more or less market value (examples; one ounce silver dollars and worthless paper, both declared worth $1; one ounce American Eagle gold coin with face value of $50).

6. Fiscal Policy: Management of government spending to fulfill obligations, and in some cases to 'stimulate', or 'guide', the economy.

7. Free Market: A market that is free from government intervention (i.e., regulation, subsidies, price controls, or governmental monopolies, etc.). In a free market, property rights (ownership of goods and services) are voluntarily exchanged at a price and terms arranged solely by the mutual consent of sellers and buyers/consumers, with no government control of pricing, creation of new firms, pay and benefits, hiring and firing, etc.

8. Gang Theft: This occurs when one group of people in some manner overpowers another group, and forcibly takes assets from them. Most people agree that it is immoral, and should be illegal, but oddly, most people believe it is OK to employ gang-theft-by-vote to tax, restrict, or control others (usually 'the rich'), via government power as the larger group sees fit. They justify it by; 'making their victims pay their 'fair share', or 'they got rich by luck', etc. **This in fact describes an immoral government.**

9. Gross Domestic Product (GDP): The market value of all final goods and services made within the borders of a country in a year. Gross National Product (GNP) is GDP plus income received from other countries (interest and dividends), less similar payments made to other countries.

10. Inflation: 1. Monetary Inflation: A rapid and excessive expansion of the money supply (such as over 5% per year; or more than growth of GNP); purchasing power of a given monetary unit (Dollar, etc.) is reduced, **2. Price Inflation:** Increase in current prices due to reduced purchasing power of money, in turn due to an increase in the money supply (or other factors such as reduced supply of goods for sale, increased demand, cartel pricing, etc.). 'Nominal' is the listed price at a given time. 'Real' is a past or future nominal price adjusted for 'price inflation'.

11. Mercantilism: An economic system where the ruling government seeks wealth, especially gold or silver bullion, by playing a protectionist role in the economy, and by encouraging exports and discouraging imports, notably through the use of tariffs, subsidies, and money valuation. The opposite is a policy of laissez-faire, which says that all trade is good and that such controls are counterproductive, and usually evolve to be used as political favors.

12. Monetary Policy: Management of the monetary system including money supply, bank reserves, interest rates, etc.

13. Money: (mostly from wikipedia.org) Money is anything that is generally accepted as payment for goods and services and repayment of debts. The main functions of money are distinguished as: a medium of exchange, a unit of account, and a store and measure of value.

Money originated as **commodity money,** then evolved to easier-to-transport representative money in which a paper certificate, or base-metal coin can be redeemed by the Bearer on demand to the Issuer (Mint). However, nearly all contemporary money systems at the national level are fiat money systems. **Fiat money** is without value as a physical commodity, and derives its value by being declared by a government to be **legal tender**; that is, it must be accepted at face value (dollar, etc.).

14. Principle: An underlying guide to thinking and action. A comprehensive and fundamental law, doctrine, or assumption. A rule or code of conduct. Dave's core political principle is: "The government's proper role is to **protect** its citizens and legal residents, as **individuals**, from threat to, or violation of, their personal and property rights by **others**". Note that; a) 'groups' (by sex, ethnic, age, etc.) have no special rights or privileges, and b) legal entities (corporations, etc.) only have property rights, but their officers may represent the personal rights of shareholders.

15. Reserves: 1. Fractional Reserve Banking means the bank need only retain a certain percent of deposits on hand (typically about ten percent) and can loan the rest. In fact, this means banks can loan ten times the amount of their deposits, thereby creating new money! For example, a $1,000 deposit can back $10,000 of new loans. **2. 'Reserve Currency'** is the money of a certain nation that by agreement or common usage; 1. can be used by banks as their 'reserve' ('good as gold') which underpins their loans and obligations, and 2. is acceptable for payments between other countries worldwide.

16. Standards for Gold-Based Monetary Systems
The gold standard is a monetary system in which the standard economic unit of account is a fixed weight of gold.

1) The **Gold Specie Standard** is the system in which the monetary unit is associated with a circulating gold coin. (issuer has 100% reserves for redemption of paper notes)

2) The **Gold Exchange Standard** may involve only the circulation of silver coins, or coins made of other metals, but the authorities will have guaranteed a fixed exchange rate with another country that is on the gold standard, hence creating a *de facto* gold standard in that the value of the silver coins has a fixed external value in terms of gold that is independent of the intrinsic silver value. An example is the Bretton Woods Agreement of 1944.

3) The **Gold Bullion Standard** is a system in which gold coins do not actually circulate as such, but in which the authorities have agreed to sell gold bullion on demand at a fixed price.

(#16-1,2,3 from http://en.wikipedia.org/wiki/Gold_standard)

4) The **Private Gold Standard** version introduced here is based on 'Redick's Four Monetary Rules' (see page 91). Under this plan, money is produced by private firms in the free market where customers (users of money) decide which type and source of money they prefer, and mints compete for customers by supplying a good product. There is no central bank (our Fed), or legal tender laws, and government mints (run by the Treasury), if any, are optional, and have no control or privilege over the private mints. The free market is allowed to work! The

144

'unit of account', and thus prices, are **weight** of the commodity (typically gold and silver) used as money. Gold reserves (in physical possession o f the mint) for redemption must be 100%, and must be published and audited.

17. Table 7: Weight: Conversion: Common units for precious metals are:

1 Tonne (metric) = 2,205 pounds (Lbs) = 1,000 Kilograms (Kg)
                = 32,150 troy oz.
1 US Ton (Short) = 2,000 Lbs advp.   =   907.2 Kg
1 UK Ton (Long) = 2,240 Lbs advp.   = 1,016.5 Kg
1 gram   = 15.43 grains = 5 metric carats = 0.643 pennyweight
1 Troy Ounce = 31.10 grams = 480 grains (gr)= 120 engl. carats
1 Troy Pound   = 12 Troy ounces (Oz) = 373.2 grams
1 Avoirdupois Lb= 16 avp. ounces= 453.6 grams=7,000 grains
1 Avp. ounce   = 28.35 grams (g), 437.5 grains
1 English carat   = 1.296 metric carats (for precious stones)

% Gold	Europe System Fineness	Carat System
100.0	1.000	24 carat
91.7	0.917	22
75.0	0.750	18

Notes:
1. The 'Long Ton' is the Imperial system used in the UK
2. The 'Short Ton' is used in the US and Canada.
3. The IMF and all nations measure their gold in metric tonnes.
4. Gold weighs 19,320 kg per cubic meter. Tungsten is close at 19,600, so it is sometimes gold plated and used as fake gold bars and ingots. Steel is 7,850, copper 8,930, lead 11,340, and water 1,000.
5. Grains, grams, and Tonne are metric units. The Troy system was started by King Henry II of England. The Avoirdupois system evolved through common usage in Europe.
6. Fineness: The purity of a precious metal measured in 1,000 parts: a gold bar of 0.995 fineness contains 995 parts gold and 5 parts of other metal; 0.999 means a coin is 99.9% pure.

4. Biography of Dave Redick

Personal: Dave grew up with his two brothers in a middle class family near Detroit, MI. When he was 14, the family moved to an 80-acre general farm near Ann Arbor, Michigan. He has an honorable discharge from the U.S. Army Reserve. After 46 years in California, he moved to Madison, WI in 2004 to be near his family.

Education and Business: Dave won a four-year tuition scholarship to the University of Michigan, based on grades, activities (Sr. Class President, sports), and need, and started in the fall of 1953. He completed his **BS-Engineering** in 1958.Upon graduation he worked as an aerospace engineer for 5 years (rocket engines and satellites) in California, and then started his career in telecom sales and management. In 1965 he earned an **MBA in Economics** from Santa Clara University in Santa Clara, CA, and after management positions in several other firms, in 1995 became **VP Sales, then President**, of a wireless engineering consulting firm www.hntelecom.com. He left in 2000 to be **VP and cofounder of a Silicon Valley telecom startup** 'Fiberstreet' (closed, see Google), and **helped raise $6 million of venture capital.** He moved to WI in 2004, and started Sustainable Energy Earth, a renewable energy engineering consulting firm. Since 2009 he has also worked as a Speaker, and Author of books, on the interaction of governments, business, people, and economics. To see my essays, go to his archive at ActivistPost.com, scroll to the bottom of the Home page, and select 'Contributors', then his name.

Political: In 1978, Dave became concerned about economic and social damage caused by government corruption, abuse, and counterproductive 'management'. He then read about and discussed this subject widely and became an activist for more cost-effective, and less abusive, government. He ran for Congress as a Libertarian in 1982 in District CA-1 (and got 3% of the vote), then returned to his Republican roots and ran again in 1984 with Reagan in the same District as a Republican (and got 38%). During the G. W. Bush administration, Dave became concerned about the Republican Party's departure from its core principles. In 2006 he was the Chm. of LPWI.org, and in 2007 the Wisconsin contact for The Republican Liberty Caucus (WI.RLC.org and RLC.org), which promote the principles of limited government and free enterprise. In 2007 Dave founded his financial website www.SaferInvesting.org. In 2014, Dave ran for WI State Assembly District. 77, and got 19% in a very 'Progressive' district where no Republican had run for over twenty years. Contact him at: RedickD@aol.com